More from
THE TEXTILE ARTIST series

Stitch, Fibre, Metal & Mixed Media
978-1-84448-762-2

Appliqué Art
978-1-84448-868-1

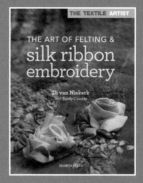

The Art of Felting & Silk Ribbon Embroidery
978-1-78221-442-7

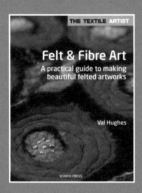

Felt & Fibre Art
978-1-84448-992-3

Layer, Paint and Stitch
978-1-78221-074-0

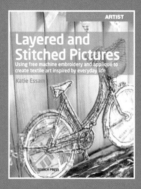

Layered and Stitched Pictures
978-1-78221-513-4

From Art to Stitch
978-1-78221-030-6

Layered Cloth
978-1-78221-334-5

Small Art Quilts
978-1-78221-450-2

The Seasons in Silk Ribbon Embroidery

DEDICATION

This book is sincerely dedicated to the golden hands of all the masters of ribbon embroidery around the world who keep on inspiring others and make our lives even more colourful, as well as to the incredibly beautiful Masters' Golden Hands (now Craft, Business & Hobby) craft show held in Kiev, Ukraine.

The Seasons in Silk Ribbon Embroidery

20 beautiful designs, techniques and inspiration

Tatiana Popova

SEARCH PRESS

ACKNOWLEDGEMENTS

To Caroline de la Bedoyere: I can hardly imagine a more valuable estimation of my work than yours. Thank you so much!
To Mary Corbet: your support is so precious, thank you for your wonderful book review!
A very special thank you to Sophie Kersey, my most patient and helpful editor. I'm so grateful for all the hard work you have done!
A big thank you to all the staff at Search Press for being so kind and helpful.
To Yuri Shumanskyi, Director of Craft, Business & Hobby International Show and Fair: that Grand Event of yours is always such a boost!
To my parents: thank you for all the lessons you have taught me.
To my favourite brother Fed Gavlovsky for his endless patience, help and all his efforts supporting our website.
Finally a very big thank you to my dearest husband, Alex Popov and sons, Gregory and Simon. Let each of you find a personal greeting sent from the pages of this book. I could not do without all your help, comfort and encouragement.

Please see the metric/imperial silk ribbon width conversion chart on page 8.

First published in Great Britain in 2019

First published by Shumanskyi Yu. V. in Kiev, Ukraine, 2016

Search Press Limited,
Wellwood, North Farm Road,
Tunbridge Wells, Kent TN2 3DR

Text copyright © Tatiana Popova, 2016

Photographs by Alex Popov and Tatiana Popova

Design copyright © Search Press Ltd 2019

Suppliers
If you have difficulty in obtaining any of the materials and equipment mentioned in this book, then please visit the Search Press website for details of suppliers: www.searchpress.com

Alternatively, the author provides her own mail-order service via her website: www.owl-crafts.com

Ready-made sets of silk ribbon for all the projects in the book and printed panels ready to embroider (where necessary) are available from the author's website and can be shipped worldwide.

Contents

Introduction 6

Getting started 8

Stitches for silk ribbon 20
  Straight stitch group 21
  Ribbon stitch group 25
  Daisy stitch group 29
  Knots 31
  Ribbon gathering 33

Traditional ribbonwork 37

Thread embroidery 45

New techniques 50

PROJECTS

Owlets 68
  Spring Owlet 70
  Summer Owlet 74
  Autumn Owlet 78
  Winter Owlet 82

Seasonal flowers 88
  Lily of the Valley 90
  Your Day 94

From Olga's Garden 102
Meadow Posy 114
Autumn Basket 120
Sunny Road 130
Christmas Rose 134
February Cup 138

Seasonal gifts 144
  Easter Wreath 146
  Mother's Day 158
  August Cup 164
  Friendship Heart 172
  Wedding Day 176
  House-warming Carp 182
  Christmas Star 188
  January Cup 192

Designs to transfer 196

Stitch index 207

Flower index 208

Introduction

In 2013 I made my writing debut. *Silk Ribbon and Embroidery*, my first book dedicated to the wonderland of ribbon stitching, was a sort of textbook on traditional ribbon art, aiming to show the joy of stitching with natural silk ribbon and to help crafters master ribbon embroidery step by step. Now *The Seasons in Silk Ribbon Embroidery*, my second book, is going to become your guide to modern ribbon embroidery styles and techniques. Here, traditions are covered but there are also innovative ideas for contemporary designs.

Colour was the phenomenon that captured me when I was making my first steps in ribbon stitching. I'm still in awe of the way in which ribbon colours interact with each other in the finished design. Silk ribbons laying flat on the table are nothing more than colourful stripes, but when they are brought together in an embroidered flower bouquet, their colour and texture speak to our artistic souls. This inspired me to base this book on the seasons, since each of them is associated with a distinct colour palette.

The title of the book has two meanings: firstly, the designs relate to spring, summer, autumn and winter. Secondly, the key note of the book is an appeal to practise ribbon embroidery all year round, since it is so worthwhile.

The overall emphasis of the book is practical. This is why some theoretical themes are merely mentioned so that you can study them further at your leisure. You will find plenty of information in other books and online. This book includes many of my own personal tips and techniques. Don't leave these out of your learning process, as they show tried and tested ways to achieve easier, quicker and more efficient stitching.

I run the Little Owl SmartCrafts company, which aims to develop the field of ribbon embroidery in art and education. Our logo is an owlet and a smiling owlet will follow you throughout the book. Every now and then I would like to smile to you from the pages of this book.

Before beginning on a project, I recommended that you read through all the instructions first. This makes things easier and will give you a good grounding, particularly if you want to make your own changes to personalise the design.

Creativity flows naturally if you are working in a field that has become second nature to you. Designs and ideas come to me from everyday life: my trips, meetings and even talks. This gives my books on ribbon embroidery an autobiographical feel, and so I wish my courteous readers a pleasant journey through the pages of my life!

Autumn Basket

The instructions for this project are shown on pages 120–129.

Getting started

The recommended sequence of work for ribbon embroidery is: choose a design, read the instructions, select materials and tools and prepare the fabric and embroidery hoops.

1 The first step is to choose a design you like. They are divided by three categories, Beginner, Intermediate and Advanced depending on the skill level needed. However, my advice is to ignore that information if you are really attracted to a particular design. The ribbon embroidery technique is different, but not difficult! In fact, some designs are called Advanced for fairly minor reasons. The variety of stitches used for a design may automatically bring it into that category even though all the stitches are very simple. Have a go – really liking the design will boost your ability. The step-by-step instructions for the projects are very detailed, which will help, so don't be put off and leave out your favourites!

2 Once you have chosen a design you want to embroider, read all the instructions first and study the stitches indicated. For most of the projects, the order of work given can be changed.

3 Next, you need to pick up the right selection of silk ribbons and iron them all before stitching. The ribbon widths in the instructions are in metric, but the equivalents in inches are given in the conversion chart (below right). While stitching, always work with a short ribbon length – 30cm (12in) is ideal – to prevent the ribbon from distorting.

4 Make sure you have the correct size chenille needles for silk ribbon and some fine embroidery needles for thread (see below). The wider the ribbon, the bigger the needle you should use to make a hole large enough to allow the ribbon to pass easily through. If not, it will damage the ribbon.

5 Now you need to transfer the picture onto the fabric. There are two options:

a If there is a pattern for the design, use a light box (or just tape the design up against the window) and trace it with any fabric marker or watercolour pencil. Try not to make too many marks or it will take a lot of time and effort to cover them with ribbon stitches. Make only a few strokes for stems and leaf veins and a few dots, ovals or circles for flower centres. All the marks will need to be hidden by stitches. Using water-erasable fabric marker makes things easier, as you can erase any lines that show after stitching.

b If the design is rather complicated, make a printed panel for it. There are designs for eleven of the projects at the end of this book (see Designs to transfer, page 196). Transfer the design onto the fabric with the help of iron-on transfer paper. Instructions are given on page 196.

6 Now take an embroidery hoop or a frame of the correct size (see page 10). Make sure your embroidery hoop will hold the fabric firmly in place while you are stitching. Silk ribbon pulls more when passing through the fabric than thread.

Ribbon width	Chenille needle size
20mm, 25mm, 32mm	13
13mm	16 or 18
7mm	18 or 20
4mm	20 or 24
2mm	24 or 26

For embroidery thread, you can use a no. 26 chenille needle or a no. 8 or 10 embroidery or straw needle.

Silk ribbon width conversion chart	
2mm	$\frac{1}{16}$in
4mm	$\frac{1}{8}$in
7mm	$\frac{1}{4}$in
13mm	$\frac{1}{2}$in
20mm	$\frac{3}{4}$in
25mm	1in
32mm	$1\frac{1}{4}$in
50mm	2in

Using embroidery hoops

Very few of us keep the whole range of sizes of embroidery hoops or frames. This means that you might encounter one of the problems described below.

Problem 1

Your hoops are smaller than your design. This is all right for most embroidery techniques, as some do not really need hoops at all. But it will not work for silk ribbon embroidery. When you are working a ribbon embroidery project, your embroidery hoop must always be big enough to allow room for the whole design. Otherwise delicate silk ribbon will be damaged while re-hooping. Moreover, it is important to see the whole design while stitching to select a proper colour shade and to assess the general look of your work.

Problem 2

Your hoops are much bigger than your piece of fabric. In fact, this is an ideal situation for silk ribbon embroidery, as you can easily fix the problem. Enlarge your fabric by attaching some extra fabric around it. Do not merely join the two pieces together with pins as shown below, left. Instead sew them together as shown below, right. The is much easier on your hands and on the fine silk ribbon.

TIP

Use the extra fabric to your advantage: it makes a perfect pincushion while you are stitching.

Threading and anchoring ribbon

Threading the ribbon

Cut a 30cm (12in) length of silk ribbon. Take a chenille needle of the correct size (see page 8) and fix one of the ribbon tails in the needle eye.

1 Thread the ribbon.

2 Pierce one end of the ribbon with the point of the needle.

3 Pull the other end of the ribbon until the ribbon is fixed in the needle.

Anchoring the ribbon at the back of the embroidery

You don't have to be an expert in embroidery to understand that we need an 'anchor' to hold the other ribbon tail at the back of the fabric. There are three ways to do this, depending on the width of the ribbon you are using. For some ribbon widths, you can use various methods.

For 2mm ribbon

Work a familiar overhand knot at the ribbon tail. Then bring the needle up through the fabric to leave the knot on the underside. This knot can sometimes be used for 4mm ribbon as well, but never for wider ribbon of 7mm and up.

For 4mm, 7mm and 13mm ribbon

Work an envelope-shaped flat knot as shown in the diagrams above. Fold about 5mm (1/4in) of ribbon and pierce it with your needle. Be sure you go through the short (folded) part first – see Start and Finish in the diagram. Bring the needle through the ribbon and continue pulling on the ribbon, until a small flat knot appears. Do not pull on the ribbon too tightly or the knot will disappear.

For 13mm and wider silk ribbon

This method involves bringing the ribbon tail to the underside and anchoring it with stab stitches using one strand of embroidery thread.

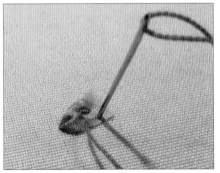

Thread a needle and fix one ribbon tail in the needle eye as described above. Take a second needle and thread the other ribbon tail, but do not fix it in the needle eye. Bring this ribbon tail from the right side of your work to the back and remove the needle. This avoids bringing the whole length through the fabric, which causes the structure of the silk ribbon to deteriorate.

Turn the fabric over and secure the short ribbon tail with a few small stitches using sewing thread.

The anchored ribbon end. Note that you should use thread of the same colour shade as your fabric. The contrasting thread has been used for clarity in the photograph.

I prefer to attach ribbon tails to the ribbon stitches on the underside of the fabric, or to join several ribbon tails together. To do this, leave a ribbon tail unfixed: just pin it temporarily in place. Having worked a couple of stitches, remove the pin. Now it is safe and the ribbon tails will wait their turn to be fixed! Make sure the same method is used to anchor the ribbon tail at the end of stitching. Never leave tails of more than 10mm (⅜in) at the back of your work. Long ribbon tails left underneath may be accidently picked up while stitching. You will find ideas for using ribbon leftovers on pages 63–64.

Controlling the shape of your stitches

Get into the habit of checking the shape of the ribbon where it comes through the needle hole every time you work a new stitch. This will give your embroidery a perfect look, which should give you joy and satisfaction.

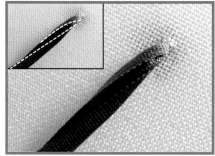

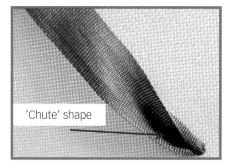

'Chute' shape

Right

All the beauty of ribbon stitches appears when they lay flat across the fabric. The photograph shows the correct shape of the ribbon at the anchor point.

Wrong

If the ribbon rolls and creates a tubular effect, your stitches will go wrong. Here the ribbon has its selvedges (the white dotted lines) folded towards its centre, so it is rope-shaped rather than flat. Bring some of the ribbon length back to the underside and take it up to the right side of the fabric again.

Wrong

Another problem appears if the ribbon comes to the surface in the shape of a chute (the red arrow in the photograph). The easy way to fix this is to turn your ribbon upside-down so that the chute faces the fabric.

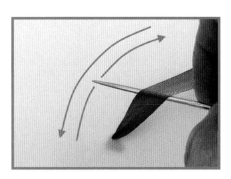

If nothing helps, use the 'ironing' method: work with your needle as shown to repair the ribbon shape. Pull on the ribbon with your non-needle hand while smoothing it with your needle. Slide the eye end of a second needle up and down the ribbon to change its shape.

SHAPING TIPS

Put the thumb of your non-needle hand on the finished stitch while embroidering the next one. This keeps its shape from distorting. Sometimes it is also recommended to Stab stitch the beginning and the end of the finished stitch in toning thread. There is no need to follow this advice every time you do ribbon stitching, just when you feel it is necessary.

Try not to stitch through the ribbon (on the right side or the back of the fabric) except when it is absolutely unavoidable.

Using toning thread, fix your stitches in the places where they should fold, twist or create any other particular shape.

Passing the threaded needle through the fabric

While working thread stitching, it is possible to bring the needle up and down in one movement (the sewing method). However, never try to do this with silk ribbon or the tubular effect appears and the ribbon looks like a rope rather than a flat tape (see opposite). For ribbon embroidery only the stabbing method works well.

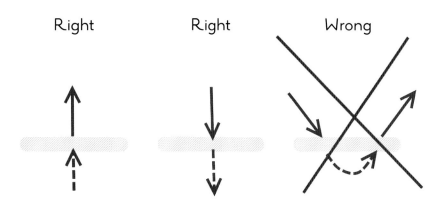

Right Right Wrong

Dyeing silk ribbon before stitching

It is fun creating your own hand-dyed silk ribbon. Firstly, it will save you money, as you will get the whole range of colours just from white silk ribbon. Moreover, it will give your ribbon a splendid colour flow which makes the stitched petals and leaves look real.

Natural silk fibre is so easy to dye, but there are one or two issues to consider. You never know the exact shade you will get, thus you have to dye more ribbon than you actually need for your embroidery design to achieve the perfect colour. The dyeing process takes time and there is a risk of hardening fine silk if you apply an unsuitable dye. To dye or not to dye, that is the question! To have the best of both worlds, use some solid-colour silk ribbon (dyed by the manufacturer) for the basis of your stock, but add some hand-dyed ribbon for more vivid designs.

What dyes to use

Special liquid dyes for silk are the best option. You can buy them in your local craft shop or online. Dharma Co seems to be the leader in that field. Marabu silk dyes also work perfectly. If you want to have a try right away and there is no dye of that kind at hand, use food dyes instead! They are made of very similar chemical components and will not harden your silk ribbon. Furthermore, you can get a whole range of dyes from your kitchen, starting from tea (black or green) and going on to different kinds of fruit or vegetable juice or herbal concoctions. But do not forget to do a test first.

Applying the dyes

When you start out, use no more than 1m (39½in) to 1.5m (59in) of silk ribbon to prevent tangling. You will be able to increase this later if needed. And don't forget to put on protective gloves before you start working!

Here are a few examples of ways to apply dyes. You will get more ideas of your own when you start practising.

Solid colour ribbon Put your ribbon into the basin with the prepared liquid dye. Leave it there for some time; the exact time depends on the kind of dye you use and the effect you are aiming for, so have a try! Sometimes it is recommended to put a metal tray with the liquid dye and the ribbon floating in it in the oven at 100°C/212°F/Gas mark ¼ for about twenty minutes, but I have never tried this myself.

Coloured sections and stains Cover your kitchen table with any kind of plastic to prevent stains. Put a length of ribbon flat on the table and apply the dyes in the colours you want in the order you want them. You can aim for a gentle colour flow or a multicoloured ribbon – both ways have their merits. It is also fun to apply some water onto the dyed ribbon to get a lighter colour here and there. Play around to find the best results.

Dyeing ribbon selvedge Fold or roll a length of ribbon and dip its selvedge into the basin of dye. Use this method to dye one or both selvedges, leaving the middle part of the ribbon undyed.

Leaving to soak

Leave the dyed ribbon to soak for at least four hours (or even overnight) to let the colours get deep inside the silk fibres. This helps to fix the colour. However, for the same reason, remember to remove any stains from your clothes while they are fresh! After this, rinse the dyed ribbon in cold water until the water runs clear to remove any excess dye. Some people find it helpful to add vinegar to the water to fix the ribbon colour. I never do this, as I haven't found it effective.

Ironing

Now iron your hand-dyed silk ribbon. It is often recommended to use a medium-hot iron, but in my view an iron on the maximum heat works better. It is not necessary to wait until the rinsed ribbon dries out completely to iron it, but make sure the wet dye does not spoil the base of the iron. Covering the ribbon with a piece of spare cotton fabric makes it safer, but it still depends on the material from which the iron base is made. Keep ironing until the ribbon dries out. The ribbon is now ready for stitching.

TIP

Wide silk ribbon (more than 20mm) often folds, twists and tangles while wet. Do not try to untie the twists right away. Firstly press the ribbon with your iron: the dried ribbon will miraculously unfold by itself. However, it will now have creases fixed by the iron. To smooth them, sprinkle the ribbon with clean water and iron it repeatedly. To iron a slightly wet ribbon, just slide it to and fro under the base of your iron: moving the ribbon is much easier than moving the iron along the ribbon length. Watch your fingers!

Dyeing leaves and petals after stitching

When your embroidery is finished, it is nice to add some colour shades here and there to the petals or leaves. You do not need to be a highly skilled artist to do this: since the ribbon stitches are three-dimensional, the light and shade areas will help you. Also, if you dye at this stage, you don't need to worry about hardening the ribbon. This doesn't matter too much in these circumstances, because the delicate ribbon folds and curls are already done. However, do be careful not to dye the fabric background! Use a hairdryer and put some paper towels under the petals to separate them from the fabric.

What dyes to use

Special liquid dyes for silk are the best option, but even ordinary watercolour paints will work. To add tiny dots to the petals or draw a leaf vein, use acrylic paints, as these are best for producing fine brushstrokes.

Choice of brush

It does not matter much what size paintbrush you use – it depends on the flower size and what you are used to.

Order of work

1 Put a paper towel under the petal you are going to dye. It will prevent the paint from soaking through to the fabric.

2 Take a flat brush and moisten the petals with clean water. You can either do this petal by petal or moisten several neighbouring petals at a time. Remember that the wet area should always be bigger than the area you are going to dye. If not, you will create unwanted marks between the dry and wet areas.

3 Mix the paints to create the right colour shade. Add some water to the mixture if necessary. Check the colour shade, for instance by painting it on to a plastic or ceramic plate. Use a fine round paintbrush to apply the paint to the petals so that the paint spreads freely around the wet area of the ribbon (see above). Be careful not to add too much colour. Remember that it is always easier to add more colour than it is to remove any excess (see opposite). If you do need to remove some, the only way is to immediately dry the petals with paper towel. However, this may not remove all the excess paint and the petal shape might be spoilt. Therefore be sure to apply pale shades of the colour first. You can easily darken the petals later by dyeing them repeatedly where necessary. Use a half-moistened brush to apply the colour so that it does not spread too much. Leave some petals or parts of them undyed. You can create wonderful, natural-looking flowers by painting the petals along the edges only, or by adding colour in the middle instead (see opposite).

4 Now it is time to get to work with your hairdryer. This will speed up the drying process, thus preventing the paints from bleeding too far into the fabric. Always have the hairdryer to hand when you are dyeing finished petals. Take care when you are using it to dry petals made from wide silk ribbon. The hot air can destroy the nicely shaped petal while it is wet, making it flat and lifeless. To prevent this, support the petals with the eye end of a second needle and do not bring the hairdryer too close to the petals.

5 Optional: apply some more colour where necessary and/or mark dots, lines, veins, etc.

More ideas for enhancing a design after stitching

These images show how the subtle application of dye can enhance your embroidery.

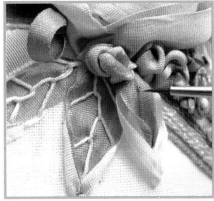

Adding small dots.

Adding fine strokes in different colours to make leaf veins.

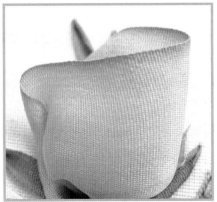

Toning the ribbon selvedge and rose petals.

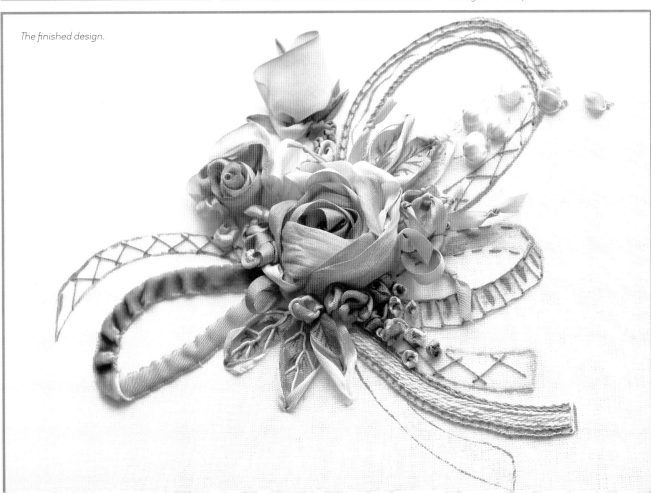

The finished design.

Colours

Nowadays we have time for leisure activities such as art and crafts. Unlike our ancestors for whom survival was constant hard work, we have the luxury of appreciating the richness of the colour spectrum. That may sound strange, but this has not always being the case. According to historian Herodotus, the Ancient Greeks had no special name for the colour blue, so in their language, the sky was called 'black'. This was not because their eyes were unable to tell the difference – they just did not see the need to create a specific word. I have found a similar oddity in the Russian dictionary. It involves the Russian name for a fox. In common with many other Slavic languages, this originates from the adjective meaning 'yellow'. Still more evidence that our ancestors had no need to create special names for all the range of different colour tones.

Modern languages, by contrast, have names for the subtlest shades of a colour. For example, yellow can be lemon, canary, honey, corn, butter, banana, daffodil, amber, golden, saffron, pineapple, straw and more. For the shades of blue we have pale blue, sky blue, azure, cornflower blue, delft blue, indigo, peacock, sapphire, berry and navy. Not to mention the shades of green, including sea green, forest green, pine and moss green; olive, fern, lime and mint green; seaweed, lettuce, pea and pistachio green; leaf green, grasshopper green and lizard green; crocodile and turtle green; parrot, emerald, shamrock or cactus green and even chartreuse. We could add dollar bill green!

I find this variety completely charming. We use the names of the familiar things around us like fruit, vegetables, berries, flowers, plants, minerals and even animals to name the colour tones. People even joke about their ability to tell the slightest variation in hue. Citizens of the Russian city of Vladivostok, where there are frequent fogs in winter, used to say, 'We can tell 140 different shades of grey!'

Perhaps everybody's favourite colours are linked to their circumstances in life. Psychologists suggest that there is always some underlying reason for the colours we choose to have around us. Keep a closer eye on this, especially as you choose colours for your embroidery and you might appreciate the colour therapy you practise in everyday life.

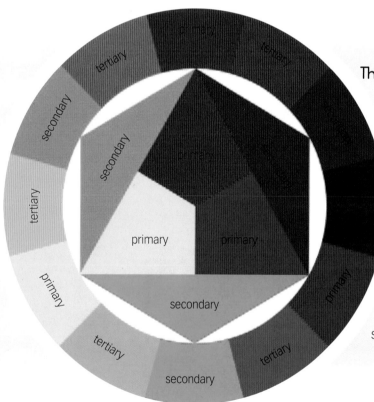

The colour wheel

You can find this described in detail online and in most books on art, photography and interior design. The three primary colours: red, yellow and blue are mixed with each other produce three secondary colours: orange, green and purple. If you mix these with primary colours, we get tertiary colours. Study simple ways of creating colour schemes based on analogous colours (next to each other on the colour wheel) and complementary colours (opposite on the colour wheel) as well as the influence of colour context. This can help you in selecting suitable colours for your embroidery designs.

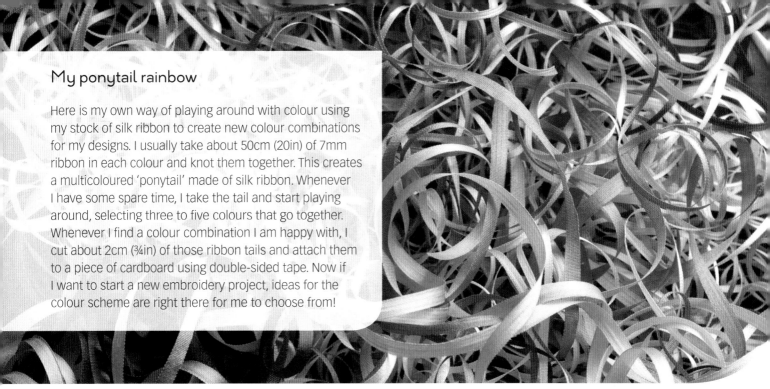

My ponytail rainbow

Here is my own way of playing around with colour using my stock of silk ribbon to create new colour combinations for my designs. I usually take about 50cm (20in) of 7mm ribbon in each colour and knot them together. This creates a multicoloured 'ponytail' made of silk ribbon. Whenever I have some spare time, I take the tail and start playing around, selecting three to five colours that go together. Whenever I find a colour combination I am happy with, I cut about 2cm (¾in) of those ribbon tails and attach them to a piece of cardboard using double-sided tape. Now if I want to start a new embroidery project, ideas for the colour scheme are right there for me to choose from!

Photographic software

We all have favourite photographs don't we? They may be family portraits, memories of trips or holidays, images of our children, or just amazing landscapes taken by photographers we know. There is a way to make them work for our embroidery needs beyond just printing them on fabric as a template for embroidery. Using photographic software, pick up colours from different areas in the photograph to make a colour card of your own. These cards can give you fresh ideas for selecting ribbon colours. Here you can see two samples from our family album. The top photograph was taken while staying with friends. Their cottage is in a very picturesque place, and it was an early morning in summer. These butterflies have a touching habit of having breakfast together! The second image shows our younger son when he was nine. He is really fond of animals and used to talk to them… and they seemed to understand him. In fact, they both seemed to enjoy themselves!

Stitches for silk ribbon

The stitches used to work the designs in this book can be divided into several categories:

Traditional ribbon embroidery stitches   I have my own guide to mastering silk ribbon embroidery in a time-honoured way, and I call it the Ribbon Tree. Students of my ribbon embroidery school have found it very effective. The forty-three main traditional stitch techniques are gathered into five groups (or branches) for easy reference: straight stitch, ribbon stitch, daisy stitch, knots and ribbon gathering. They are found on pages 21–36.

Traditional ribbonwork techniques   These mostly involve ribbonwork using wide silk ribbon (see pages 37–44).

Thread embroidery stitches   These are very simple stitches that many of us will have known since childhood (see pages 45–49).

My own particular ribbonwork techniques can be found in the next chapter, New techniques (page 50).

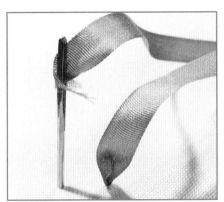

Straight stitch

This stitch needs no introduction or explanation: the photographs show perfectly how to start out and work the Straight stitch. Remember this stitch while learning Central ribbon stitch (page 25), as it is very helpful to compare them!

Arched straight stitch and Looped straight stitch

The diagram shows three variations of a straight stitch: lying flat across the fabric, raised above the fabric like an arch, or shaped into a loop. These loops are really useful for stitching beautiful flower petals. To make them the same size, work them around a knitting needle or pencil (see the white arrow in step 1). You can also place the loops flat, Stab stitching through their base to secure them, as shown in steps 2 and 3.

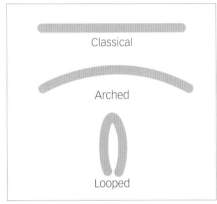

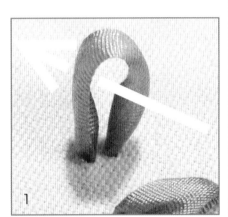

Eye-looped stitch

Work a loop and flatten it across the fabric, attaching a seed bead or working a French knot in the middle. In the photographs it is shown using the head of a sewing pin for clarity.

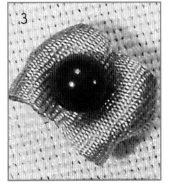

Twisted straight stitch

Twist your ribbon once to create a twisted leaf (right) or repeatedly until it becomes a smooth tight tube for a flower stem (steps 1 and 2 below). Bring your needle to the back (step 3). Finally, work Running stitch in toning thread with short stitches going through the stem and long stitches on the back of the fabric (see Twisted ribbon stitch, page 26).

One twist to make a twisted leaf.

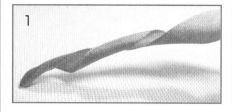

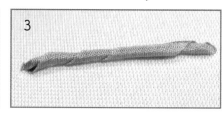

Rope technique

Bring the ribbon out (1) and twist it tightly. Fold it in half and let both halves twist around each other. Poke your needle back down next to where it came up (red point A in step 4) and knot or fix its end to prevent untwisting. Ropes make nice stems, stamens and bird feathers. Placed side by side in rows, they make neat baskets.

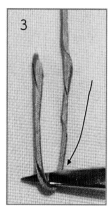

Twirled ribbon rose or Rope rose

Twist about 10–15cm (4–6in) of ribbon- tightly. Fold it in half and let both halves twist around each other. Poke your needle back down next to where it came up (red point A in the photograph) and pull on the ribbon carefully until a nice small rose appears. Secure it with a thread, going through the centre, or attach a seed bead (the red dot in the right-hand photograph).

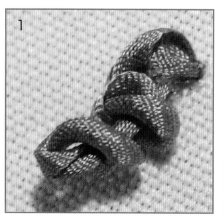

Whipped straight stitch and Crescent rose

Whip a Straight stitch with the same ribbon to add more texture. Let your ribbon go flat. This method works nicely for creating rose petals as shown below.

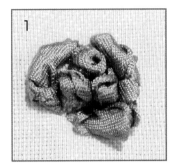  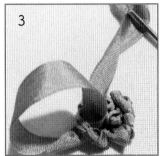 

Folded straight stitch

Work an Arched straight stitch (page 21) and fold it at an angle as shown. Secure the fold in place using a toning thread.

Padded straight stitch

Simply work two or three Straight stitches on top of each other. Each stitch should be about 1mm ($\frac{1}{32}$in) longer than the previous one.

TIP

Save ribbon by working the first stitch from left to right and the next from right to left, avoiding long stitches on the back of your fabric.

Couched straight stitch

Work a long Straight stitch – up to 30cm (12in) and attach it to the fabric with any thread stitch.

Straight stitch.

Two options for stitching to couch the Straight stitch down, with French knots (left) or Herringbone stitch (right).

Small bow stitch

Work a Loop stitch (page 21). Fold the top half of the loop down to flatten it so that it forms two smaller loops on both its sides. Work a short Straight stitch across the centre of the loop to secure it in (steps 3 and 4). While mastering this stitch, you can use a pin to fix the bow shape temporarily.

 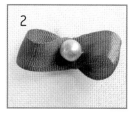  

TIP

Add some ribbon tails to the bow, as shown in the photograph (left). Simply bring a short length of ribbon through the second stitch. For clarity the photograph shows ribbon tails of a contrasting colour, but they would normally be the same colour as the bow.

Big bow stitch

Follow the step-by-step photographs below. The contrasting blue ribbon in the final step and the sewing pins have been used for clarity.

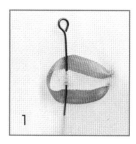 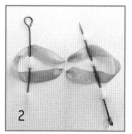 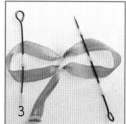  

Plume stitch

Work an Arched straight stitch (page 21). Take the needle back down, then bring it up again, poking through the first stitch. Continue stitching in this way until you get a plume of the required length. The last stitch of the row is not an arched one; it should be a classical flat Straight stitch to fix the other loops in place. This stitch looks great in hand-dyed ribbon!

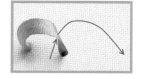

Above: working plume stitch.

Left: the three pictures show the worked plume from various angles.

Ribbon stitch (centre ribbon stitch)

Centre ribbon stitch is often just called Ribbon stitch. Bring the needle up to the right side and take it down THROUGH THE RIBBON before it passes through the fabric (see step 1 below). Pull on the ribbon, allowing it to curl at the tip (step 2 below). These curls are typical of Ribbon stitch and give it its charm. It is easy to experiment to get the effects you want. Pulling on the ribbon just a little, you will get a mallet-shaped stitch (see below). I call it this because it reminds me of a croquet mallet (right). If you continue pulling on the ribbon, the stitch will become pointed, as shown in the photographs below, right. Usually, when Ribbon stitch is featured in instructions, it does not matter which kind you work. I would rather not treat the mallet shape as a separate stitch, but as a Centre ribbon stitch variation. Bear in mind that if no specification is given in the instructions for the mallet shape, Ribbon stitches are normally expected to be pointed.

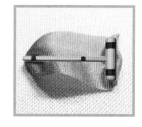

The reason I call the flat-tipped ribbon stitch a 'mallet-shaped' version.

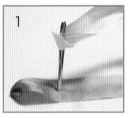

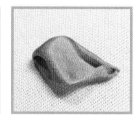

A mallet-shaped Centre ribbon stitch.

A pointed Centre ribbon stitch.

A more pointed version of the stitch.

Arched ribbon stitch

Compare the two stitches in the photograph: the blue one (laying flat) is the usual Central ribbon stitch and the green one is an Arched ribbon stitch.

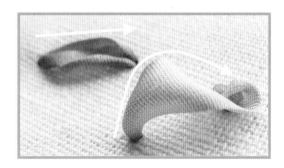

Looped ribbon stitch

If you work a loop in Ribbon stitch, a nice flower petal appears. Silk ribbon embroiderer and author Ann Cox used this stitch to make the five petals of a nasturtium. Place the ribbon curls (formed at the tip of Ribbon stitch) inside flowers to add charm to ribbon loops.

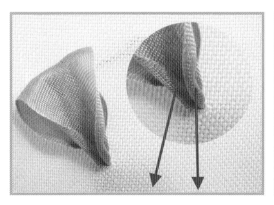
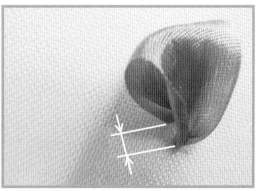

Looped ribbon stitch. The arrows show the two curls at the tip.

The white arrows show the space that should be kept to a minimum as for Looped straight stitch (see page 21).

Reverse ribbon stitch

Normally ribbon curls (formed at the tip of Ribbon stitch) face upwards. They are the distinctive decoration of Ribbon stitches. Reverse ribbon stitch is different: its curls face the fabric. They raise the stitch above the fabric, thus creating a beautiful effect. The stitch can be worked using two methods.

Method 1

Fold the ribbon at an angle and pass the needle through the ribbon and the fabric in one movement, as shown below.

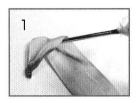 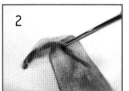 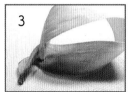  

The finished stitch.

Method 2

Take the needle up through the ribbon, not touching the fabric. The black circle on the first photograph indicates the place for the stitch. Tighten the loop, and only then pass the needle through the fabric.

Both methods will give the same result, so choose whichever you like.

 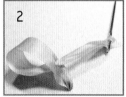 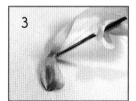 

The finished stitch.

Twisted ribbon stitch

The only difference between this and Twisted straight stitch is that it has ribbon curls at the tips. In fact, these curls don't really work as decoration, as they are too small. However, they help to fix the stitch in place before we pin it or Stab stitch it with thread. That is why I often use it instead of Twisted straight stitch. Fix the twisted stitch using thread. To make this easier, work longer stitches on the back of the fabric and tiny stitches along the right side as shown by the yellow line.

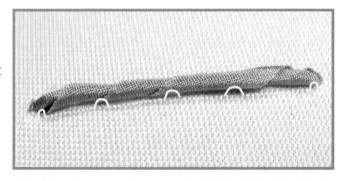

TIP

Try to make just one or two twists, and this will make a nice leaf.

Side (right or left) ribbon stitch

For Central ribbon stitch, the needle goes through the centre of the ribbon width. This version is different: it goes through the place near the ribbon selvedge on the right or left (depending on whether you are working right or left ribbon stitches).

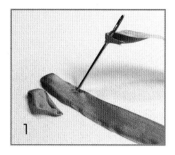

Half-bow stitch

This is a personal invention of mine. I had already been using it for a year or two when I found a similar stitch called Shortened ribbon stitch, and this alternative name may help you to master it. I first worked this stitch because I was tired of embroidering time-consuming Eye-loop straight stitches.

Follow the steps below: bring the needle up to the right side of the fabric, then take it down to the back VERY CLOSE to the first point (step 1). Do not forget to LEAVE A RIBBON ARCH (the first loop) on the right side. Without pulling too tightly on the ribbon, form a second ribbon arch (the second loop) as shown in step 2.

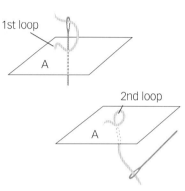

1st loop

A

2nd loop

A

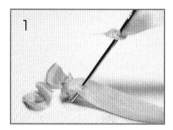

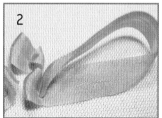

Three stitches worked.

Double ribbon stitch

Take the needle down through the ribbon as usual, but do it twice: the first time do not go through the fabric (step 1), just pulling it tight to fix the curls. Then go about 1mm (1/32in) from the first point (as if shortening the stitch) and pass the needle down through the ribbon and the fabric together (step 2), as for Central ribbon stitch. Longer ribbon curls will form at the tip of Double ribbon stitch. Sometimes this stitch is even better than the usual Central ribbon stitch: its shape is more similar to the natural shape of certain petals such as some types of chrysanthemum.

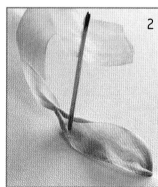

Folded ribbon stitch

Firstly fold the ribbon at an angle – any angle you like. Then pierce it, forming the usual ribbon curls at the tip. You can fold the ribbon as shown in the photograph (the tip with curls is UNDER the main part of the stitch), or do it vice versa (the tip comes OVER the main part of the stitch). But do not forget to fix the folds using a toning thread.

TIP

Use a sewing pin to support the fold until it is fixed with thread (see the photograph, left).

Raised ribbon stitch (Ribbon stitch on a stem)

This stitch can be either pointed or mallet-shaped.

Mallet-shaped

This version is more difficult to perform without explanation, so it is shown in three steps. Use a second needle to shape the curl, then pass the needle down through the fabric. Now pull the stitch tip up, holding the second needle. The 'stem' that is formed will be almost invisible if you are looking at the embroidery from the front. But it will help to create a splendid 3D effect, with raised petals.

TIP

To hide the stem, you can give it a little twist. This makes it narrower and so easier to conceal. This is good for front rose petals.

Pointed

For the pointed variation, work a Ribbon stitch curl as for Double ribbon stitch (not going through the fabric). Pull it tight and then take the needle down through the fabric, leaving a short stem on the right side. This works well for sunflowers and chrysanthemums.

The pointed version of Raised ribbon stitch.

Rudbeckia ribbon stitch

The stitch itself was first found in Ann Cox's book on ribbon embroidery *The Handbook of Silk Ribbon Embroidery.* I call it this because she used it for rudbeckia petals. Another rather cumbersome name for it is 'Ribbon stitch worked with the ribbon folded in half along its length'. Use either 7mm or 13mm ribbon. Fold it in half widthwise so that the two selvedges meet. Now work the usual Ribbon stitch, piercing down through the two layers of ribbon and then the fabric (see the photographs). This creates a more textured stitch. Observe flowers in nature to help you choose which petals to use this stitch for.

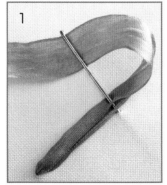

Lazy daisy stitch (classical)

Work a loop, then bring your needle up through the fabric inside the loop and work a short Straight stitch to secure the loop in place. Play around, varying the length of the loop and stitch to create different shapes. Changing the ribbon size is also fun.

Twisted daisy stitch

Work the same way as for Classical lazy daisy stitch above (a loop, then a short Straight stitch to couch it in place), but twist the loop before couching. This will provide more texture. This stitch works nicely for rosebuds. Try different ribbon width for more options!

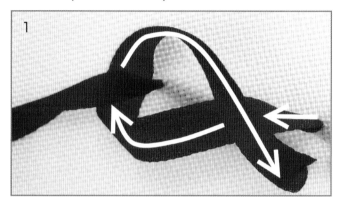
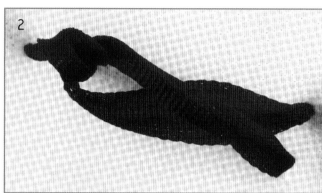

Fly stitch

This is a Lazy daisy stitch variation, with the initial loop being open. Vary the length of the fixing stitch for different shapes or twist it to create a stem with two ribbon leaves formed by the two halves of the loop.

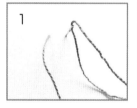
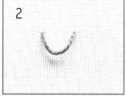
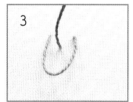
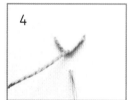

The finished stitch.

Grab stitch

This is often used for the combination of flower cups and stems. Work the usual Lazy daisy stitch, but do not finish it. Place the securing stitch sideways rather than in the usual direction (see the photographs).

The finished stitch.

Spider web rose (also known as Woven wheel)

Spider web rose is featured in the Daisy stitch group due to the fly stitch used to form its web.

The web

Method 1: Use Fly stitch to work a spider web base for the best-known ribbon rose. Work a Fly stitch first (shown in blue thread), then add a Straight stitch inside the Fly stitch (the red arrow). The result is five rays of spider web, radiating from the centre. The web in the photographs is worked with thread, but it is better to do it with 2mm silk ribbon in the same colour as for the rose petals.

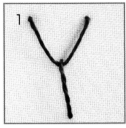 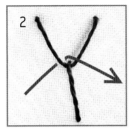 

The finished spider web.

> **TIP**
>
> *it is important to fix the stitches properly on the back of your fabric to prevent damaging the rose.*

Method 2: This is the traditional way of stitching the spokes with five straight stitches, but I prefer method 1.

  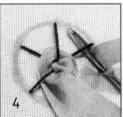

The rose petals

Change to 4mm, 7mm or 13mm ribbon. Starting from the centre of the circle, weave over and under the five spokes without going through the fabric (see step 4 above). Because you are working with an uneven number of spokes, the next time you come around the circle you will be going above the stitches you went under last time, and vice versa. It is important that each spoke alternates under and over or the rose comes out misshapen. Try variegated silk ribbon or use different colours to work this rose. Vary the ribbon size – for instance use 7mm ribbon for inner and 13mm for outer petals.

The finished rose.

Knotted daisy stitch

A nice, interesting, yet rather complicated stitch. To stitch it for the first time you will need 7mm ribbon, time and patience!

The finished stitch.

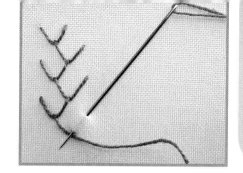

Feather stitch

This appears if you work Fly stitches to the right and to the left side of the stitch line in turn. Perfect for seaweed! It may form a feather-shaped line or an irregular spider web (being worked in a random order).

French knot

This is a popular and well-known stitch. It can have one, two or three wraps round the needle). Follow the photographs to master it. Play around with ribbon size and the number of loops to create different sizes of French knot.

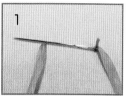
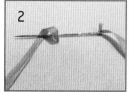
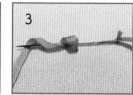
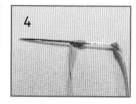

TIP

Be careful when pulling on the ribbon to finish the stitch. You want a nicely tightened knot without any of the loop left loose. Tighten the smaller loops first and then start pulling carefully on the bigger loop.

The finished French knot.

Pistil stitch

If you move away from the place where the ribbon or thread comes out of the fabric before making a French knot, it will become a pistil stitch. The name originates from the botanical name of a flower part, which it resembles. It is especially good for fuchsia pistils and stamens.

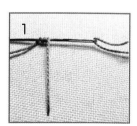
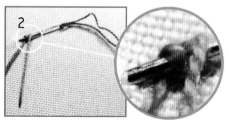

TIP

There is a small thing you can alter when working Pistil stitch. Start by placing the silk ribbon either above your needle (see the green arrow in the left-hand photograph) or under your needle (see the orange arrows in the right-hand photograph). Usually it doesn't matter much, but sometimes it changes the placement of the knot. Try both to see which you prefer.

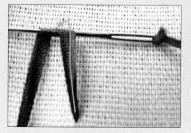

Colonial knot (also known as English knot)

This is a twisted stitch resulting in a knot, similar to a French knot. I love it and often use it instead of French knots. It seems to be easier to pull on the ribbon evenly so that no loop remains in the finished Colonial knot.

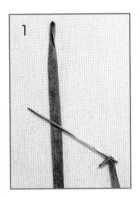

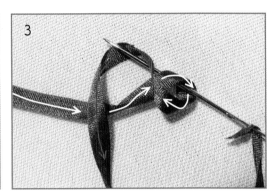

Star rose

This stitch can be worked using either Colonial knots or French knots. I prefer doing it with Colonial knots. Work a Colonial knot at least 7cm (2¾in) from the start. Using the same needle, work Running stitches along the 7cm (2¾in) of ribbon. Take the needle down to the back of the fabric and tighten the knot.

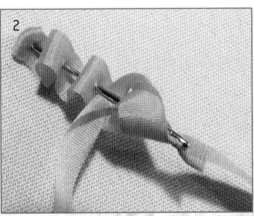

TIPS

· *If all the loops go in the same direction, twist them to shape the rose (see the red arrow in the photograph).*

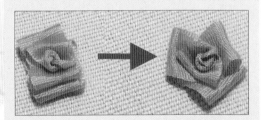

· *While working Running stitches, try to make each next stitch a little longer than the previous one, so that the rose's bottom petals are bigger than those in the centre of the flower.*

General rules for ribbon gathering

• These classical gathering techniques are not usually applied to 2mm or 4mm silk ribbon: use them with 7mm and wider ribbon only.

• Always try to work Running stitches as small as you can make them without getting bored! This rule becomes even more important for 7mm or 13mm ribbon.

• There are two methods for ribbon gathering – study both to work out which you prefer:

Anchored method

The gathering is worked along a ribbon length that is anchored to the fabric. Thread a chenille needle with a length of silk ribbon and fix it in the needle's eye. Secure the ribbon tail to the fabric with matching thread and tiny Stab stitches (see Anchoring the ribbon tail at the back of your embroidery, page 11). Note that these Stab stitches should be covered with the gathered ribbon afterwards. Using the same thread, work a line of Running stitches according the pattern of gathering you have chosen. Having finished, bring the thread to the back of the fabric and secure the gathering in place according to your design. Now bring the needle and ribbon to the back and secure the ribbon tail in the usual way. (I prefer this way of stitching; but some embroiderers find working the very beginning of the line of Running stitches inconvenient).

Non-anchored method

The gathering is worked along a ribbon length that is NOT attached to the fabric, and having finished, you bring the ribbon tails to the back of your embroidery.

Cut a length of ribbon the right length for gathering + 3cm (1¼in) extra, allowing for the ribbon tails to be brought to the back. Bring the threaded needle through the ribbon 1.5cm (⅝in) from the end and work Running stitches, following one of the gathering stitch diagrams on the following pages. Finish working a row of Running stitches 1.5cm (⅝in) from the other ribbon end. Pull the thread to gather the ribbon as tight as you want it. Fix the thread but do not trim it. Now bring the ribbon tails to the back of the fabric using a chenille needle of an appropriate size. Secure the gathered ribbon in place with the same thread.

When using the non-anchored method of gathering, you will be more comfortable working the Running stitches, but you might have some problems bringing the ribbon tails to the back of the fabric. Leaving longer ribbon tails will help to some extent, but you will have to use extra ribbon.

• Make sure you fix the gathering thread properly at the beginning of the line of stitching. If the knotted thread tail slips through the hole in the ribbon while you are pulling the thread to gather your ribbon, all the stitches will be lost. To prevent this, work one or two tiny stitches over the ribbon edge before you start working gathering stitches as shown in the photograph below.

• Always use one strand of thread to work gathering stitches. Choose thread that matches your ribbon.

• Try to hide fixing stitches inside the ribbon folds and place them along the line of gathering stitches to make them invisible.

• If you are using the anchored method of gathering ribbon, there is no need to knot the ribbon tail before stitching. Anchor the ribbon to the fabric with tiny Stab stitches like the ones you work to secure your thread.

• On the following pages you will find different gathering stitch diagrams. Use all of them to work the samples. This will help when you come to use them for your designs. I have developed the names to help you to master and remember the stitches.

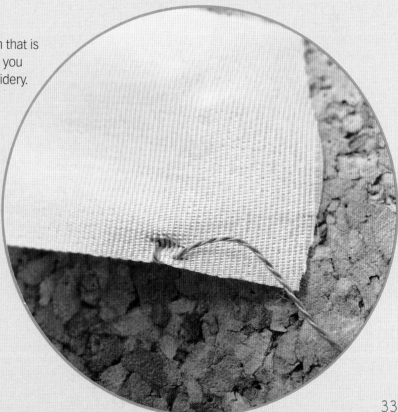

Ruche gathering

Work Running stitches along one of the ribbon selvedges. Pull on the thread to gather the ribbon. It can form a nice fuchsia, a daffodil cup, or thousands of other things! Tighten the gathering as much as you need and use ribbon of different sizes and colours to suit your particular requirements.

Jabot gathering

This stitch reminds me of jabot decoration used for dress embellishment. Embroider a line of Running stitches along the centre of the ribbon middle. Pull on the thread to gather the ribbon. This works nicely for catkins, ribbon leaves or petals.

34

Zigzag gathering

Anchor the gathering thread to the ribbon selvedge, then work the gathering stitches crossing the ribbon at 45°, referring to the diagram. For the best result try to keep to the same angle all the way along. Making marks with fabric marker along both ribbon selvedges may be helpful, but is not essential. When you have finished, pull the thread to gather the ribbon: you will get nice scallops that will sit either side of the Running stitch. Secure the gathered ribbon in place with matching thread and tiny Stab stitches, trying to hide these in between the folds.

TIP

Zigzag gathering in an oval shape. Pass the needle through the fabric and come up again inside the oval. Work another oval, just a little smaller then the first one. Its scallops should lay on top of half the width of the first oval scallops.

Go on until all the shape is filled. This makes a nice double rose, marigold or dahlia. You can make circles instead of ovals, or even work a long gathered length and shape it into a spiral. Zigzag gathering is also good for fish scales or bird feathers.

Cherry blossom (or Sakura) gathering

This stitch got its name for its ability to create a life-like fruit tree blossom. Work the gathering stitches along the ribbon, referring to the diagrams. Try to place the slopes of each peak (stitches coming across the ribbon) as close to each other as possible, but do not let them interfere with or go through each other. It is always a question of how far apart to space these peaks. (Once gathered, each of these spaces will form one flower petal). To get natural-looking, rounded petals, keep to the rule that the space should be about twice the ribbon width. This is a very approximate formula, however: the space may vary by up to 2mm. If you stitch Sakura with a much longer space left between the peaks, your petals will look rather like a trapezium – but this is fine if it is what you intend. Play around to see which shape you want to get. The diagrams below show the pattern for a five-petal cherry blossom flower (the numbers indicate the order of stitching petals for right-handed stitchers).There are two options (see the General rules for ribbon gathering on page 33): try both methods and choose your favourite. The difference is whether to stitch the first and the last slope of the pattern or not. There is no need to do it for the anchored method. It gathers the beginning and the end of the ribbon length with the threads of the fabric itself.

Peak

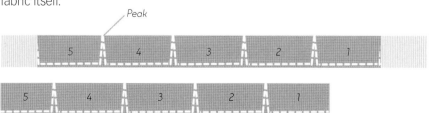

Non–anchored method

Anchored method

One slope sakura

Work Running stitches along only one slope of every hill. This will pull your flower petals into propeller shapes, and it will also save you time. The diagram shows the order of stitching for right-handed embroiderers. Work the Running stitch right to left. Work the first horizontal line; go up the first vertical slope. Now the dotted red line breaks, but do not cut the thread. Jump to the bottom of the next dotted line and follow the same order of stitching as before.

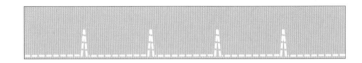

Low hill sakura

Work Running stitches in toning thread, following the diagram. Do not make the hills too high, they should not reach the other ribbon edge, as this makes all the petals look joined together rather than separate.

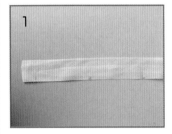
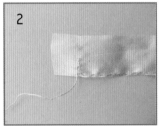
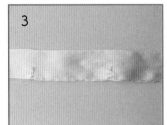

Rounded slope sakura

Work a line of Running stitch as shown in the diagram. Make sure it is rounded. The peculiarity of this kind of ribbon gathering is that it allows you to create both petals (marked A in the diagram) and a sort of flower stem (marked B). This is why the stitch is popular for embroidering lilac blossoms.

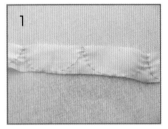
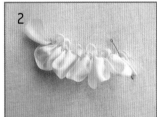

Traditional ribbonwork

Classical twisted rose (or Rolled ribbon rose)

The photographs show a simplified way of working this rose. Use 13mm or any wider silk ribbon. Fix both the ribbon tail and the thread in the centre of the rose (photo 1). Go around the centre to make a kind of ribbon roll and stab stitch it at the bottom (2 and 3). Now slightly twist the ribbon tail and place the twisted ribbon around the rose centre, stab-stitching it here and there as you wish (4 and 5). Go on until the rose is of the required size.

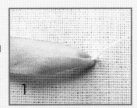
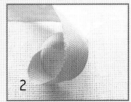

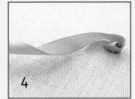

Bow on a fork technique

Follow steps 1–6 below to make a bow. The classical way of creating a bow is to weave across the fork prongs five times. Then the bow will have four loops and two ribbon tails. Fix the bow using a second length of ribbon: insert this between the two middle prongs of the fork and tie it in a knot (the yellow ribbon in steps 7–9). The bow can easily be turned into a nice little flower such as a violet. To do this, you wil need a fifth loop, as violets have five petals. Weave across the fork prongs for the sixth time to make the extra loop. Now either bring the ribbon tails to the back of the fabric or trim them off on the right side, then hide them under the petals.

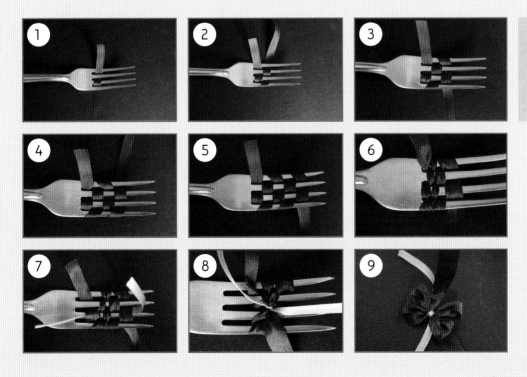

TIP

Play around with the bow colour and size: bows have so many uses!

Cabbage leaf technique

Usually used with wide silk ribbon (at least 13mm wide). Cut about 5cm (2in) of 13mm silk ribbon. Pin with pins or use the eye of any big chenille needle to make winding easier. Insert the ribbon corner into the needle eye and roll the ribbon. When the roll is finished, twist the needle gently and take it out of the roll. Having finished one roll, fix it with a pin and wind on the other side. Work Running stitch along the bottom edge. Make sure you stitch through the rolls so they do not come undone when you remove the pins. Pull on the thread as tightly as you wish to gather the petal to the desired shape. Fix the thread and trim off. Cut off the excess ribbon tails.

TIP

Experiment, varying the angle at which you wind up the rolls, up to almost vertical. Note the difference this makes to the shape of the finished petal.

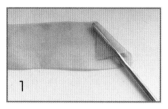

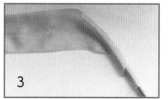

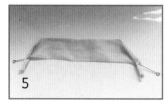
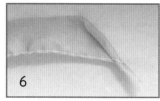
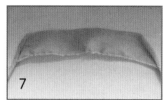

Belt technique

Take a length of silk ribbon at least 13mm wide and work Running stitch across its width using toning thread (1). Stitch to and fro three to five times. Do not forget to pull on the thread every time one pass of Running stitch is completed, to gather the ribbon. Hide the thread tail in the ribbon folds and trim the thread (2). Fold the ribbon in half so that the stitched area is below the fold (3). Hide the ribbon tails under the flower centre (4) or bring them carefully to the back of your embroidery. This helps to create charming dimensional petals.

TIP

It is better NOT to tie a knot at the end of the thread before you start stitching. Just leave a thread tail of about 2.5cm (1in), do the stitching then trim it off at the end of the work.

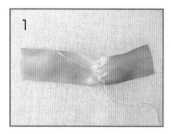
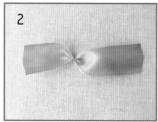

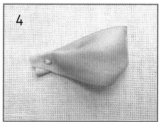

Tent technique

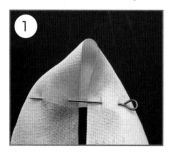
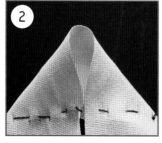
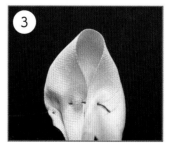

Fold the ribbon as shown in step 1 and gather as shown in steps 2 to 3. This stitch is ideal for tiny rose leaves (see page 77).

Wide ribbon rosebud

Inset pictures show the reverse side.

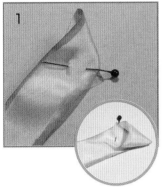 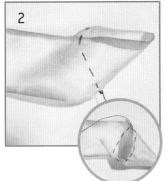 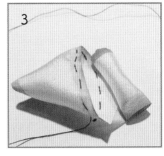 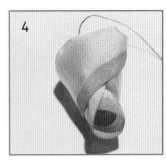

Half-cabbage leaf technique

Take a short length of wide silk ribbon (ribbon leftovers work fine). Roll one of its corners at 45° as shown in step 2. Work Running stitch along the two other sides of the triangle (step 3). Be sure to fix the thread properly at the beginning of the line of Running stitch. Pull on the thread to gather the ribbon, and you will get a nice 3D flower petal (step 4).

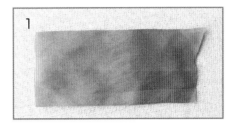 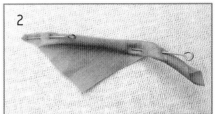

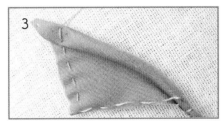 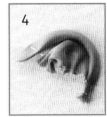 

Double tent technique

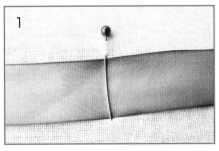

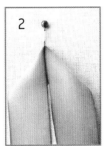 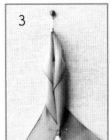 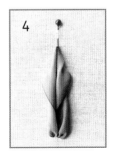

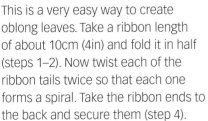

This is a very easy way to create oblong leaves. Take a ribbon length of about 10cm (4in) and fold it in half (steps 1–2). Now twist each of the ribbon tails twice so that each one forms a spiral. Take the ribbon ends to the back and secure them (step 4).

Triangles in a square technique

This technique involves folding ribbon into a packet and then gathering it. The way to fold the ribbon is shown in the photographs immediately below, using striped paper for clarity. It is quite easy except for the fact that silk ribbon is very fine and does not retain folds the way paper does. For this reason, you will need pins to keep the ribbon in place, as shown further down the page.

YOU WILL NEED

12cm (4¾in) of 20mm silk ribbon or if working with wider ribbon, a piece 1–2cm (⅜–¾in) longer
Sewing pins
A cork board or similar

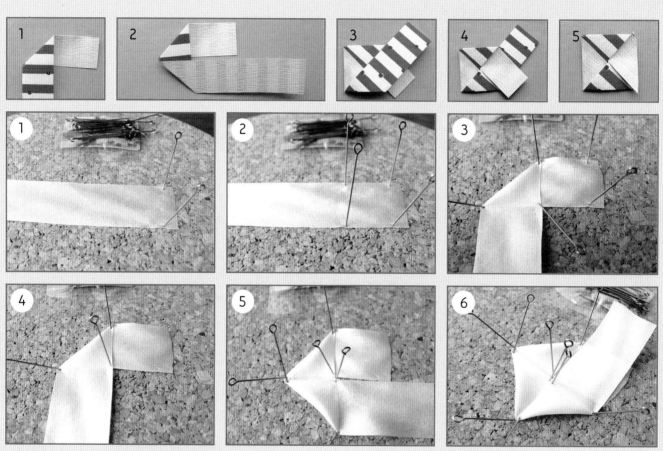

1 Begin by pinning the tail end of the ribbon onto the cork board as shown.

2 Place third and fourth pins as shown, to create a square of pins. These will be known as the vertical pins.

3 Work the first fold at right angles to the ribbon tail. Fix it with pins as shown.

4 Now remove the first two pins – they are no longer necessary.

5 Continue folding and fixing. Be sure to place the pins only in the corners and centre of the square or the delicate silk ribbon might be damaged.

6 Having reached the stage shown, weave the two ribbon tails together. The sequence above in striped ribbon shows you how in steps 4 to 5.

7 Before you start working the Running stitch, fix the folds using pins that do not pierce the cork board but just go through the two layers of ribbon as shown. It is important to place one of these horizontal pins before taking the vertical pins away. The folded ribbon should now be taking on a square shape.

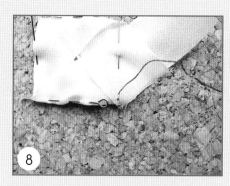

8 Work a line of Running stitch around the edge of the square. Start stitching along the side where the two ribbon tails meet. Use one strand of toning thread (contrasting thread is shown for clarity). Knot the thread tail but do not trust the knot – it might easily slip through the fine ribbon threads. To avoid this, work several Stab stitches at the very beginning of the Running stitch. Try to work in very small stitches about 2mm (1⁄16in) long for a neat result.

9 This photo shows a threaded needle instead of a sewing pin along the two ribbon tails. This is where you start the Running stitch. Continue along the other three sides of the square in a similar way.

10 Now the Running stitch is finished, pull on the thread to gather the ribbon. The flower (or bud) is ready. The red arrow in the inset photo shows the asymmetrical part of the bud. This is fine but should be taken into consideration when you are attaching the flower/bud to the fabric.

To make anchoring easier, work Stab stitches whilst the bud is half open. As is usual for all the gathering techniques in silk ribbon embroidery, the Stab stitches should go through the parts of the ribbon where Running stitch was placed.

Two-sided Janus technique

This is my own technique. The name originates from the Roman god Janus who had two faces. The technique is worth using when, for whatever reason, we need to double the length of the stitching ribbon. Normally this should be 30cm (12in), otherwise the ribbon will become distorted with repeated stitching through the fabric. Sometimes, e.g. while stitching the petals of a sunflower, it is better to use a 60cm (23½in) length so that you have fewer ribbon knots or tails at the back. Cut 60cm (23½in) of ribbon and thread both ends into chenille needles (1), like the two heads of Janus! Now bring both needles to the right side of the fabric close to each other (2 and 3). Firstly stitch with one needle, placing stitches clockwise (4), then use the second needle to stitch flower petals counterclockwise (5–6). Step 7 shows the back of fabric.

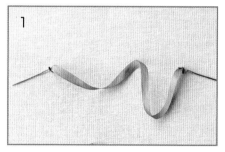

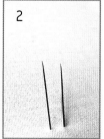

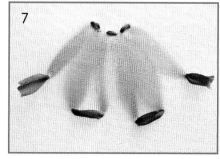

41

Knotted flowers

The best options for this technique are using 7mm variegated or hand-dyed silk ribbon. Experiment to find out what works best for you.

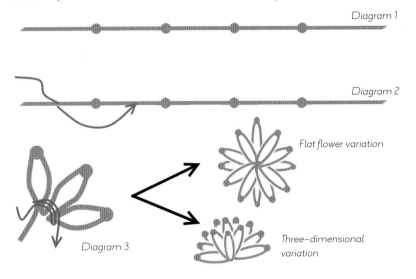

Diagram 1

Diagram 2

Flat flower variation

Diagram 3

Three-dimensional variation

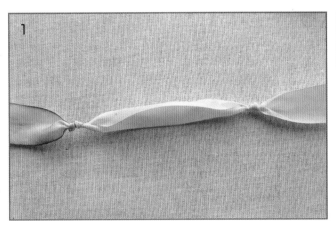

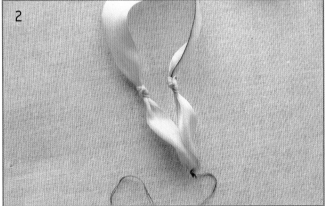

1 Take some 7mm ribbon and work overhand knots along its length. Leave 5–7cm (2 to 2¾in) space between the knots. Use something to measure the space, e.g. a chenille needle (Diagram 1). Put the needle on the table, place the ribbon length along it and start tying the knots: one at the eye end of the needle, another at its point. Go on until the desired length of knotted ribbon is reached. Do not forget to leave about 2–3cm (¾–1¼in) free ribbon at both ends. When the flower is finished, you will bring these ends down through the fabric to attach the flower to your embroidery.

2 Using toning thread, sew through the knotted ribbon as shown in Diagram 2 (the green arrow). To make it easier, fold the ribbon in half, so that the two neighbouring knots come together. Then work several Stab stitches at the fold to fix it.

3 Repeat with the next folds (Diagram 3). Go on until you have worked a flower. It can be either three-dimensional or flat.

TIP

Work the same knotted flower pattern with green ribbon and it will make good greenery for a landscape or brooch.

Button rose technique (also known as Flat rose)

1 All you need is a 30 to 40cm (12 to 16in) length of wide silk ribbon, 20mm or more, and a 2.5cm (1in) diameter circle drawn on a piece of fabric. You can also use any material like foamiran, which is commonly used to make artificial flowers, instead of fabric. Cut out a foamiran circle, work a rose and then attach it to the fabric.

2 Knot one ribbon end and then attach the knot to the fabric in the very centre of the circle with Stab stitches. Work the stitches on both sides of the knot as marked with white dots. The thread shown in the photograph is too heavy for your stitching. It is used here for clarity. Use one strand of any kind of toning stranded cotton thread.

3 This shows the small Stab stitch. Do not forget to cut away the extra ribbon tail (see inset circle).

4 This shows the direction of the first circle of rose petals. Keep folding round and round anticlockwise.

5 After making each fold, fix the ribbon in place with a tiny Stab stitch along each of the ribbon selvedges.

6 Make your next fold. See the tiny Stab stitch: only the ribbon selvedge is supposed to be attached to the fabric.

7 Do not place the ribbon flat when working a petal. Form a crease as if folding the ribbon in half along its selvedges so that they are almost touching.

8 Turn the ribbon upside-down every time you make a fold for a new petal. Do not worry about making the petals look different: as both sides of taffeta silk ribbon look the same, there should be no difference.

9 Continue in the same way until you get a rose of the desired size. You can place the petals close together or leave some space in between so that the whole flower looks bigger.

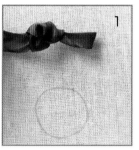

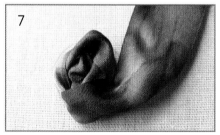

Puffy petals

This is my own method.

Diagram 1: The blue outline shows where the petal will go.

Diagram 2: The red line marks the loop stitch from A to B. Make sure B is 1cm (³⁄₈in) away from the end of the petal).

Diagram 3: The purple lines show Stab stitching to fix the ribbon loop in place.

1 To embroider a petal, cut a length of ribbon 2cm (¾in) longer than the petal itself.

2 Bring one ribbon tail to the wrong side of the fabric where you want the petal to start (near the flower centre – A in Diagram 2).

3 Thread your chenille needle with the second ribbon tail and bring it to the wrong side about 1cm (³⁄₈in) from the petal end (B in Diagram 2). This folds in the end of your petal by 1cm (³⁄₈in). Do not pull the loop too tight.

4 Pin the end of the petal to the fabric. Be careful not to pin through the ribbon, or you might damage the delicate silk. Look at the pin on the fold of the petal in the photograph above: it holds the ribbon in place without going through it.

5 Now fix the shaped petal in place. Stab stitch the folded part of the ribbon in small stitches, using silk thread (see Diagram 3).

The pink arrows show how to fix a pin on the fabric.

The violet arrow shows where to fix the ribbon temporarily at the beginning of a petal.

44

Thread embroidery

Running stitch

Whipped running stitch

1

2

3

4

Whipped backstitch

Backstitch

1

2

3

4

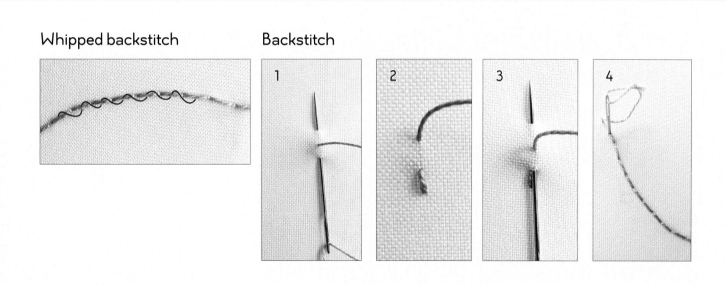

Stem stitch

Whipped stem stitch

1

2

3

4

1

2

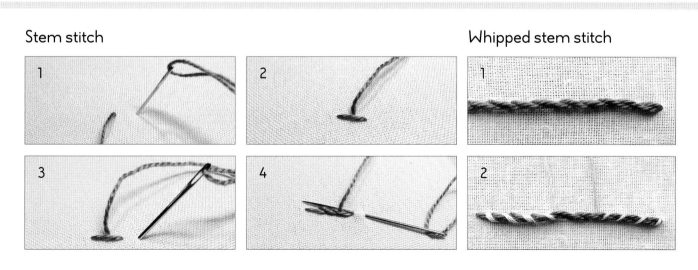

Raised stem stitch

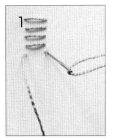 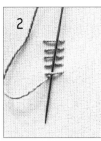 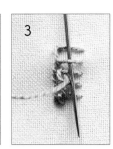   

Split stitch

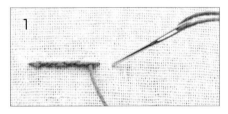  

Chain stitch

Whipped chain stitch

Open chain stitch

Long and short stitch

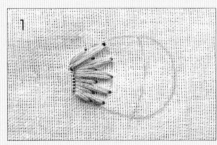  

First row

Work embroidery, alternating long and short Straight stitches. Drawing in stitch guidelines first helps to create a neat end result.

Second row

Change the thread colour, e.g. to a lighter hue of the previous one and fill in the gaps, but this time work long stitches only. Keep to this rule for all the other rows except for the last.

Final row

Stitch, alternating long and short stitches again to fill in the gaps in the previous row.

Weaving stitch

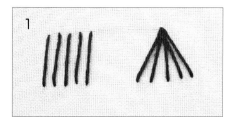
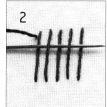

Word long straight stitches as your warp threads. Weave over and under with your weft threads (2) Work your way back, going under the threads you went over before. Continue, alternating in this way.

Open fishbone stitch

This stitch is useful if for example you want to embroider openwork translucent lacy leaves for the background. Start with a Straight stitch going along the leaf vein from the tip of the leaf. Go on working, as shown in the diagrams, gradually coming down along the central vein of the leaf until all the leaf is stitched.

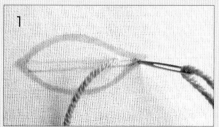
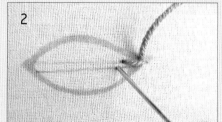

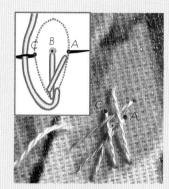

TIP

Having mastered Open fishbone stitch, it is easy to work the alternative, Raised fishbone stitch (above). Compare the placement of C and A for both stitches (either on the leaf edge or inside the leaf, along its central vein).

Buttonhole stitch

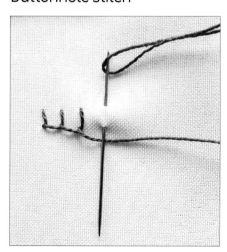

Tassel stitch

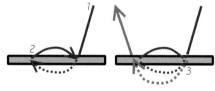

1 Following the blue arrow, bring the threaded needle from the right side to the back of the fabric and come again to the right side close to where you started. (The dotted part of the blue arrow shows the movement under the fabric).

2 Following the red arrow, bring the needle to the back again where you started.

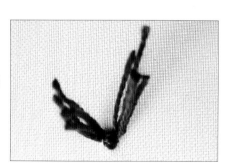

3 Following the green arrow, go through the fabric at the second point and bring the needle to the right side of the fabric again. You will get a sort of tassel protruding through the fabric. Trim away the threads, leaving a short tassel.

Woven circle filling needlelace

This is also called Woven circle filling. This kind of needlelace might seem laborious, but it is actually fun, so enjoy it!

1 Make marks at about 5mm (¼in) intervals. You can use sewing pins or a HB pencil. Do not use water-soluble marker or the printed panel might be damaged while dissolving its lines.

2 Work supporting threads. Make them double, but take care they do not twist together. Work Straight stitches. Try to start and finish all the stitches in the blank area around the printed panel. This will make the edge of the panel look neater.

3 Stitching in one thread only, work the lace itself as shown in the diagrams below.

4 Optional: decorate the lace by working Straight stitches in 2mm ribbon and couch them with French knots. If the ribbon becomes twisted due to multiple French knots worked one by one, there is no need to iron it. Just moisten it a little and it will become flat again. If you moisten it too much so that it is wet, wait a little until it dries. Working with wet ribbon is difficult and does not seem to give such a nice result.

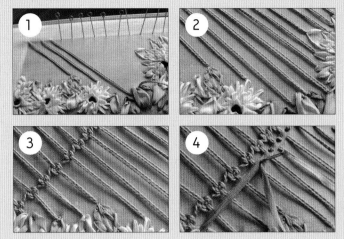

The diagram (above right) shows one intersection of the lace only. The numbers indicate the weaving order. Make sure that the double thread that forms the basis of the lace is placed above the working thread EVERY time. The green arrow indicates the way your thread goes from one woven intersection to the next. Make sure the direction alters each time to make your lace look neat.

Crochet chain

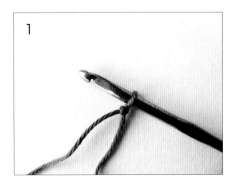

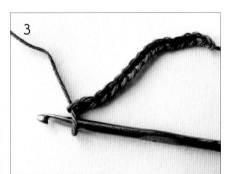

Tuning fork stitch

This is my own method. The diagram above shows the sequence of stitches in rainbow colours: start from the red one and go down the stem. For a lazy version of this stitch, see page 60.

1 Pay attention to the filling stitch for the 'tuning fork' which starts the row.

2 The two-coloured stitch indicates Fly stitches in pink and blue.

Trapunto embroidery

Attach some extra fabric underneath the chosen part of your design from the back of the work. You can pin the extra piece in place first, then work a line of Backstitch, Stem stitch or Split stitch around the area and trim off excess fabric (2). Carefully make a cut in the extra fabric (3) and fill in the 'pocket' with cotton wool, felting wool or another filler (4). Sew up the cut. Now you have a nice three-dimensional element on the right side of your embroidery (bottom right).

TIP

It is important not to put too much filling in the 'pocket' or the surface of your embroidery will be distorted. Make a habit of checking the general look of the work from the right side before sewing up your 'pocket'. If there are any creases or folds, remove some of the filling.

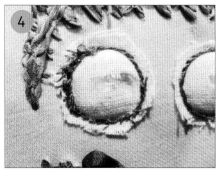

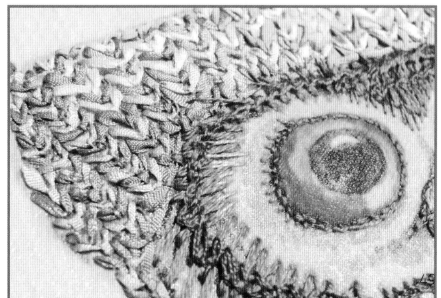

The finished effect from the right side of the embroidery.

New techniques

I have developed all the techniques described below to achieve new textural effects in ribbonwork and to make silk ribbon embroidery easier. I hope they will help you too!

Ribbon plus technique

Two lengths of ribbon are used here: one for support and the other for stitching. This method helps you to create puffy flower petals without using thread to fix them in place.

1 To prepare before working the flowers, work Straight stitches around the flower using a supporting ribbon, one for each petal. The stitches should be placed across the petal right at the tip (see the red lines). The wider the petal, the longer the stitch.

2 Work the Straight stitches in a circle around the flower, as if working a running stitch. The dotted lines show the ribbon on the back of the fabric; the solid lines show stitches to go on the right side of your embroidery. The arrow shows a possible direction of stitching. It does not matter whether you work clockwise or counterclockwise. When you have finished, trim off the ribbon and fix the ribbon tail at the back of the fabric. The supporting stitches can also be worked with thread, but it does not give such a good result as the tips of thread stitches are seen through the ribbon stitches, spoiling the look of the embroidery.

3 Now work the petals. Use the stitching ribbon to work one, two or even three stitches for each petal. Work either Straight or Ribbon stitches. Go over and under the supporting stitch every time. The arrows in steps 3 and 4 show two alternative directions of stitching. Practise both to see which one you prefer. Following the green arrow direction makes it easier to control the ribbon tension and shape the petal.

4 Following the blue arrows makes it possible to work a nice Ribbon stitch placed towards the flower centre. In this example, the flower centre is a Star rose (see page 32).

TIP

You can use this technique for any flower, even daisies with their narrow petals. Just work very small supporting stitches across the petal tips. Thread two needles with lengths of ribbon: a stitching one and a supporting one. 7mm or 13mm ribbon are often used for stitching and 2mm ribbon for support.

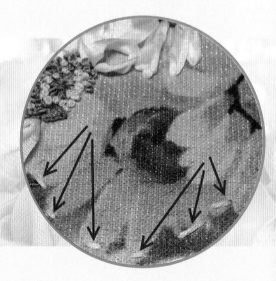

Victoria Amazonica technique

Victoria Amazonica is a name of the biggest water lily in the world. It originates in South America. This wonderful plant can carry up to 50kg (110lb) in weight, and locals use its leaves for boats! The lily got its name in 1837 in honour of the young Queen Victoria who came to the throne at that time. The leaves of the lily have a high vertical border around the edge. The scroll that is formed by this stitching technique looks very similar, which is how it got its name.

The main advantage of this technique is that it helps keep the shape of mallet-shaped Ribbon stitches without fixing them with thread. The technique can be applied to everything from leaves and flower petals to fish fins! You will need two lengths of ribbon: one for stitching and one for support. The classic combination is to use 7mm ribbon for stitching and 2mm ribbon for support, but play around with ribbon sizes, for instance, using 2mm ribbon for both purposes gives a totally different yet charming result!

It is important to choose both ribbons in one colour, otherwise the supporting ribbon might be seen through the stitches. If you want to make a multicoloured leaf and change the colour of stitching ribbon during the embroidery process, you should change the colour of the supporting ribbon as well.

The Victoria Amazonica technique is used for the dorsal fin on this fish. The technique is shown step by step overleaf.

The Victoria Amazonica technique is shown right: work a Ribbon stitch, placing the supporting ribbon inside the ribbon loop. This prevents the loop from distorting. Make sure the supporting ribbon remains on the right side of the fabric until a row of stitches is finished. Then it is brought to the back of the embroidery and anchored properly.

The tip of a leaf

There are some particular issues when stitching the tip of a leaf with this technique. The step-by-step images below show how to achieve it.

1 Place the stitching ribbon flat on top of the tip of the leaf.

2 Using the supporting ribbon, work two Straight stitches at an angle, coming through the stitching ribbon.

3 Now change to the stitching ribbon again. Work a Ribbon stitch using the stitching ribbon, so that the needle comes through the fabric at the point marked by a red dot in the photograph. Pull on the ribbon until the loop is fixed. The pointed end of the ribbon stitch now comes exactly where the leaf tip is thanks to those small stitches in supporting ribbon. The only problem with these leaves is that they often have a gap along the central leaf vein. One solution is to cover this space with a rope worked in Twisted straight stitch, as shown right.

Eyelash technique

This stitch really looks like beautiful long eyelashes! I strongly recommend you use a length of ribbon of 15cm (6in) or even less. Using sharp scissors with long blades, cut one of the ribbon selvedges. Fray the ribbon along the cut line, removing threads until you get a fringe of the desired length. This works perfectly for flower stamens, feathers or other kinds of decoration. Experiment: try cutting and fraying both ribbon selvedges.

TIP

Try combining ribbon of different colours for flower stamens – it works perfectly! Attach the fringe to the fabric with short Stab stitches using toning thread.

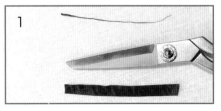

Dyeing the eyelashes

Dying the fringe creates wonderful results. There are two ways to do this.

Method 1) Apply the dye before fraying; you will get a coloured stripe along the fringe.

Method 2) Apply the dye onto the finished fringe (laying it flat, for instance on a plate). Lift the fringe from the plate while it is still wet. Some of the fine silk threads will stick together. The effect reminds me of faded flower stamens or dishevelled bird feathers.

TIP

Keep the silk threads that came from your frayed ribbon for birds' nests, tree trunks etc. Just gather them together by rubbing them with your fingers and then attach them to the fabric with thread.

Kokeshi doll technique

This technique is based on Ribbon stitch, sometimes known as Japanese ribbon stitch. The stitches are placed inside each other, which reminds me of a Russian doll. The Japanese have similar dolls called Kokeshi, and that is how the technique got its name.

Work three Ribbon stitches, one on top of the other, so that the first stitch is the longest and the last is the shortest. Use silk ribbon of different widths: 7mm for the bottom stitch, 4mm for the middle stitch and 2mm for the top stitch. Make all the stitches pointed. Let the first stitch lay flat on the fabric, place the next one on top of the first, slightly raised and the last stitch should be Raised ribbon stitch. See the numbers within the red square for the order of stitching. This technique works beautifully for both flower petals and feathers!

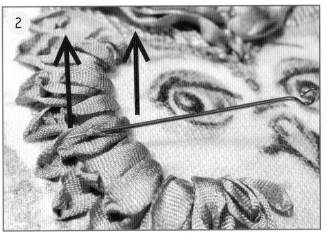

Lazy ruche technique

This is a quick and easy way of gathering ribbon with no thread stitching needed. The key is pulling on the threads correctly. But first you need to get the threads out of the ribbon.

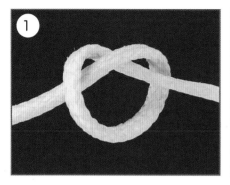  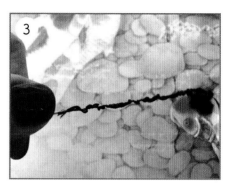

1 **The knot** Take a length of ribbon 15 to 20cm (6 to 8in) long. Knot one end tightly in an overhand knot (shown above in thread). Thread the other ribbon end into a needle (without fixing it in the needle's eye) and bring the ribbon to the right side of the fabric. The knotted ribbon end remains on the back of the fabric. Remove the needle.

2 **A tassel becomes a fringe** Fray the ribbon end a little until a small tassel appears. Now brush the tassel with your needle so that it becomes a fringe. All the threads of a tassel stay together so that it is impossible to tell which of them goes along the ribbon selvedge (which we need to know for the next step). In a fringe, the placement of the threads in the ribbon becomes obvious. Note that there is no need to fray a tassel into a fringe for 2mm silk ribbon, as this is so narrow that it does not matter which thread you pull.

3 **Pulling the thread** Grab several threads from the fringe with your index finger and thumb and pull. It is not easy to catch these fine warp threads, so some people prefer to use tweezers. Make sure you grab several threads, not just one, as this will help strengthen the construction, and the fine silk threads might break if you pull just one. Pull to gather the ribbon. Note that If you grab and pull on the threads along one ribbon selvedge, you get a Lazy ruche gathering, while pulling the threads along the middle of the ribbon produces Lazy jabot gathering.

4 **Attaching to the fabric** Fix the gathered ribbon on to the fabric in short Stab stitches with toning thread. Stranded cotton thread works fine.

TIPS

· *This method of gathering produces a very delicate result that will need more careful fixing with thread. However I have checked: if well attached to the fabric, it will usually survive washing and may be used for embroidering a blouse or dress. Just use 2mm toning ribbon instead of thread to attach the ruche to the fabric.*

· *Never use too long a ribbon for Lazy ruche technique, as the fine silk threads might tear.*

· *Do not forget to knot one ribbon end as described in step 1 above.*

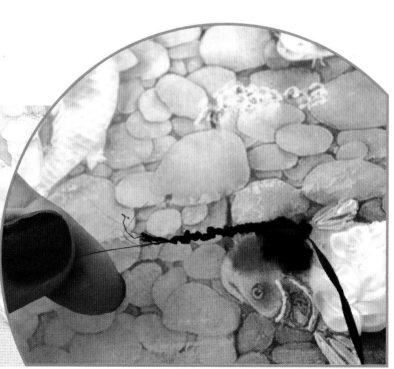

Lazy double ruche technique

This technique makes totally impossible things possible if compared to classical Ruche gathering! The work order is very similar to the Lazy ruche technique. The only difference is that you are pulling on threads going along both ribbon selvedges, so you gather the ribbon along both sides. This is a wonderfully simple way to create a lovely textured ribbon. What's more, it would be impossible to achieve this with, for instance, a 4mm ribbon in the traditional way by sewing Running stitch along its selvedge.

This stitching technique looks nice in any ribbon size. For example, in 4mm ribbon it helps create a tiny textured line (see the photograph). Attach the gathered ribbon to the fabric with tiny stitches in a toning thread. Note: work these stitches as shown by the red lines, not in blue ones. This will save time and help to hide the Stab stitches.

Another nice option is to sew Lazy double ruche using 13mm ribbon and attach it to the fabric in one-wrap French knots worked in 2mm ribbon.

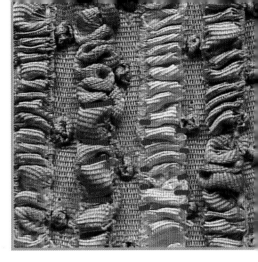

There-and-back technique

The name comes from the change in the direction of stitching. Two different stitches are united for this technique: Ribbon stitch (A to B) and Straight stitch C to D. The only difficulty is to make the BC space minimal, otherwise the stitch will not look as attractive. I recommend leaving a loop in your ribbon (loop 1, at B), so that the space near point B is still accessible.

Come up at A and work a Centre ribbon stitch between A and B, but do not tighten loop 1. Now the needle is at the back of your fabric. Press on loop 1 with your finger, placing it out of the way of point C. Now bring the needle and ribbon to the right side at C, very close to B, about 1mm (¹⁄₃₂in) away. Having brought the threaded needle up through the fabric, do not take your ribbon all the way to the right, but leave another loop (2). Now tighten the loops: firstly pull on the loose ribbon (1) to fix the pointed tip of the Ribbon stitch on the right side of the fabric. Then tighten the loop underneath the fabric (2). Now finish the Straight stitch through D, about 1mm (¹⁄₃₂in) beyond A. This method has three advantages: it is nice and textured, it produces very little ribbon on the back of the fabric and it is very well fixed. You can even use it for stitching clothes!

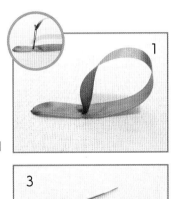
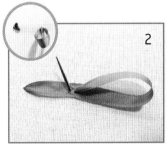
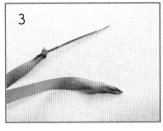
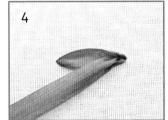

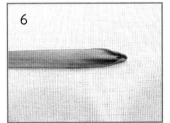
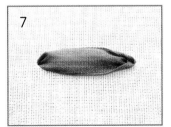

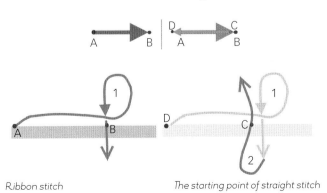

Ribbon stitch

The starting point of straight stitch

Plumeria technique

I associate the shape of this stitch with the tropical plumeria flower. Work a Reverse ribbon stitch (see page 26) and let it become arched. Roll some more ribbon over the second needle, which is supporting the loop of the Reverse ribbon stitch. At present the loop is placed perpendicular to the stitch. Turn the second needle so that the roll goes at an angle to the stitch. Now the stitch takes on a rhombus shape, which suggests a plumeria flower petal. The only difficulty is that the stitch needs to be fixed with thread straight away or its shape can be distorted. However, we have made a nice unusual petal in one movement, which is excellent!

Great Wall of China technique

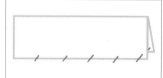

I named this after the wall partly because of where silk comes from, but also because its shape recalls that long weaving wall! Bring a length of 13mm ribbon to the right side of the fabric. Fold it in half along its length. Thread 2mm toning ribbon and work small Stab stitches through both selvedges of 13mm ribbon to fix them on the fabric. In this way, you can work a straight or a curving line or even a spiral. It is possible to sew a 'wall' of any length! This technique makes a beautiful border for flower petals or any other sort of decoration. It may also be used to embroider a dress or blouse.

Wasp waist technique

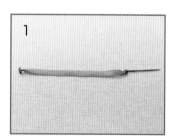

As its name suggests, this technique is all about forming a narrowing across the ribbon width. First of all, remind yourself of a Ribbon stitch and how it is formed: the ribbon comes through itself and is then brought to the back of the fabric. This is just a little bit different. Place the point of your needle in the centre of the ribbon. Pass the needle through the ribbon but NOT through the fabric (2). Pull the ribbon to tighten the loop: a narrow part like the waist of a wasp will be formed (3). Fold the ribbon in half so that the wasp waist is on top of the loop (4). Finally, bring your needle down to the back of the fabric, keeping the pointed loop on the right side. The tip of the loop will not fray so this is a perfect way to create three-dimensional petals without cutting them out from silk ribbon.

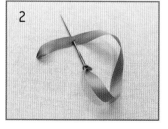
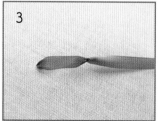
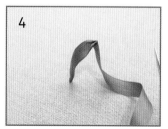

Flood filling technique

This technique is used to fill in a flower petal or a leaf with ribbon, as if you were pouring the ribbon into the shape. The ribbon will spread around the area, creating nice folds.

Using a toning thread, fix one of the ribbon selvedges around the contour of the detail (e.g. a leaf), so that the ribbon outlines the leaf. Depending on the ribbon size, either bring theribbon tails to the back of the fabric or hide them under the folds.

The other ribbon selvedge is folded inside the element and then fixed with thread. There are dozens of ways to do this. Play around and develop your favourite method.

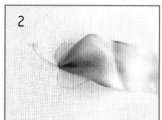
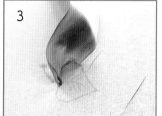

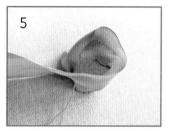

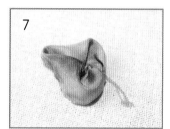

Braid technique

There is nothing difficult about this technique, which just features common braids using three lengths of ribbon. But how wonderfully it works!

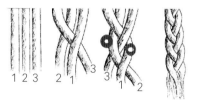

1 2 3   2 1 3   3 1 2

Starting

4mm ribbon seems the best option for this technique, but play around and be creative! Knot all three lengths of ribbon together with an overhand knot. Thread one of the loose ribbon ends into a chenille needle of the appropriate size and bring it to the right side at the starting point of the braid. Now bring the second and third ribbon ends through in the same way, anchoring them separately.

Plaiting

Now start plaiting. Work in the usual way. Take care to create a regular plait. Pin the braid to the fabric to see whether it is placed properly. If you are happy with the result, stitch it to the fabric with toning thread, trying to hide the stitches inside the braid. One more important detail: the red circles in the diagram (above, right) show where the ribbon should be turned upside-down to make the surface of the braid smooth. Luckily, there is no difference in the look of the two sides of taffeta silk ribbon so it does not matter which faces up.

Finishing

To fix the other end of the braid to the fabric, bring all three ribbon tails to the back of your embroidery and attach them using a toning thread. Another option is to fix them from the right side and trim off as shown in the photograph – but this is only possible if this area is going to be covered with another element of the embroidery.

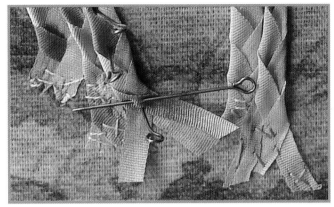

Ribbon colour

Play around with this for braids; there are plenty of possible colour combinations. Using ribbons of three different colours seems to work best. Working a braid in one colour is also beautiful and subtle. I don't tend to like the 2 + 1 pattern, by which I mean using two ribbons of the same colour and the third different. However, in some circumstances, it might work for you.

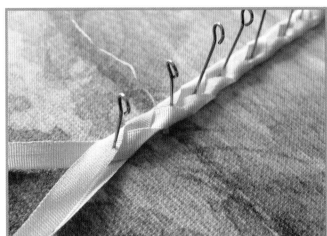

Whipstitch finishing

Natural silk ribbon is of course very delicate, but you can create beautiful three-dimensional elements with it. This is just one of the options for finishing your ribbon selvedge.

Use 7 or 13mm ribbon for stitching and 2mm ribbon to finish the ribbon selvedges in Whip stitch. Work an Arched ribbon stitch in 7 or 13mm ribbon, bring the needle back and trim off. Now thread 2mm ribbon and start working the Whipstitch along one of the ribbon selvedges, as we usually do with fabric to prevent it fraying. Having come to the tip of the Ribbon stitch, go to the back of the fabric. Repeat along the other ribbon selvedge. Be sure not to go through the fabric while stitching in 2mm ribbon – the idea is to stitch around the ribbon selvedge only, to strengthen it and add texture.

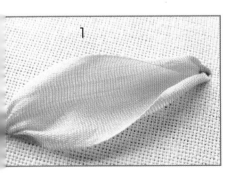

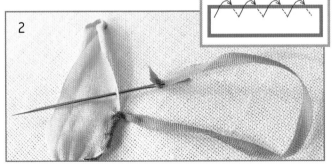

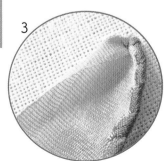

Hemisphere technique

This method works for stitching spherical elements like berries, apples, oranges or round flower buds. Usually, when it is necessary to create a hemisphere in ribbon embroidery, a bead is attached to the fabric. Then the bead is covered with a number of Straight stitches. But this means that every time you want to stitch a berry or a flower bud, you need to go and get beads from your craft shop. The alternative is to keep a stock of these beads in different sizes, and they had better not be too expensive, as they are going to be covered with silk ribbon. Good for you if you have a ready supply of beads, but I don't, which is why I've thought of a way to stitch a berry without using them.

Work a French knot and then cover it with a series of Straight stitches. It is important to preserve the hemisphere shape of the knot while stitching (see the diagram, below right). Make a French knot with one, two or three loops, depending on the size of the flower bud you want to make. Then cover the knot with one, two or three Straight stitches. Make sure you start and finish stitches UNDER the knot. This will keep the shape of the bud rounded. If you start and finish the Straight stitches beside the knot, the bud will look like a rice grain, not like the round bud of lily of the valley, for instance. The photograph at the top of the page shows lily of the valley buds. For this project, see page 90.

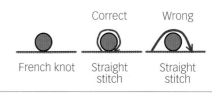

TIP

Use a second needle to keep the ribbon flat while making Straight stitches. Twisted ribbon does not work for this technique.

Lazy tuning fork technique

Tuning fork stitch got its name from its shape (see page 49). Compare the two following simplified ways of working the stitch, A and B. Each has its advantages. Use both in your embroideries as you like.

A) Work a row of Backstitch and then sew loops of Tuning fork, anchoring them to the next Backstitch as shown below.

B) Work a Couched straight stitch (1–3 below) and add the loops, anchoring them at the points of couching (4–6).

Option A is fine if you need to stitch a curved line, while B works better for straight lines. Both of them allow you to create the two-coloured Tuning fork stitch: the middle part (say, the line of Backstitch) may be worked with thread of one colour, while the loops are worked with thread of another colour.

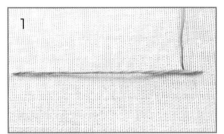
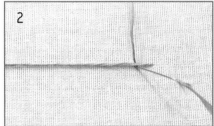
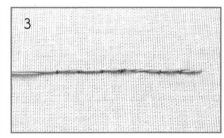
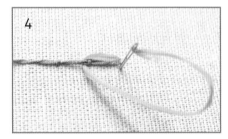

False bullion knot technique

You will notice that all these stitches are a bit counterfeit, being either 'lazy' or 'imitation'! An overhand knot is familiar to everybody. We often use it to secure thread or ribbon tail at the back of the fabric (see the first diagram, right). If several loops are worked for this knot (see the second diagram) and then pulled tightly, it forms a shape like Bullion stitch. This technique is a real treasure for ribbon embroidery, as it enables you to create a Bullion type knot wherever you like without any risk of distorting the ribbon. Two or three knots worked in sequence make a beautiful flower centre for pansies.

Vertical line technique

The ribbon goes in two planes: horizontal and vertical. Work a Looped ribbon stitch in 7mm ribbon. Go to the back of your embroidery. Bring the ribbon up again about 1mm ($\frac{1}{32}$in) to the right of the anchor point of the looped ribbon stitch. Fold the ribbon in half along its length and wrap it around the looped ribbon stitch as shown in steps 2 and 3, taking the ribbon down about 1mm ($\frac{1}{32}$in) to the left of the same anchor point. Thus you will surround the Looped ribbon stitch with a vertical border.

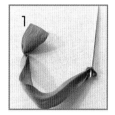  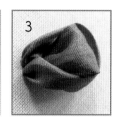   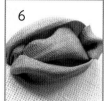

Hood technique

This is the way to work the big sunflower leaves for the Autumn Basket design on page 120.

1 Cut a 10 to 15cm (4 to 6in) length of wide silk ribbon – 20 to 32mm (¾ to 1¼in) wide.

2 Fold the ribbon in half widthways. Whipstitch the selvedges, connecting them together (see the light green arrows in the diagram) with fine toning embroidery thread. The length of the Whipstitch should be equal to the ribbon width.

3 Turn the stitched hood inside out. Put it flat on the fabric, the hood laying under the two ribbon tails. Now it is time for the most exciting job: attach the ribbon tails to the fabric, gathering them in a freeform manner (see the photograph).

TIP
Do not bring the ends of the ribbon tails to the back if you can hide them under neighbouring leaves.

Goose foot technique

The three small stitches on top of the wider ribbon remind me of a goose foot. Work a Centre ribbon stitch with 7mm silk ribbon and fix its base with three shorter Ribbon stitches using 2mm ribbon. Use the same colour for both ribbons. Contrasting ribbons have been used here for clarity.

Right angle technique

The shape of this finished embroidery technique reminds me of the well-known fitness exercise shown here! Use 20mm silk ribbon. Work Running stitch (page 45) to create Zigzag gathering (see page 33) about five to seven spikes long. For classic Zigzag gathering, you attach the gathered ribbon to the fabric flat. With this technique, half the ribbon scallops lie flat and the others stand up.

1 Work the gathering stitches using one strand of toning thread. Make sure the Running stitches come close to the selvedge, or even go over the ribbon edge.

2 Decide how tightly you want the ribbon to be gathered. The photographs show two options.

3 Both photographs show flowers created from the gathered ribbon, which is attached to the fabric in a circle, using Right angle technique. The blue marks were made to show the scallops standing up vertically while the white ones stay flat on the fabric.

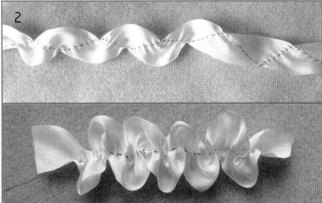

This side view shows the right angle more clearly.

Using silk ribbon leftovers

It is important to keep pincushions in order, so it is better if chenille needles do not remain threaded after stitching is finished. If you unthread them, though, you will end up with a huge pile of ribbon leftovers. At first glance, these odds and ends might look useless – but look again!

Firstly sort out your silk ribbon leftovers into the following categories:

(1) short leftovers: 2–13mm ribbon less than 5cm (2in) long;
(2) long leftovers: 2–13mm ribbon more than 5cm (2in) long;
(3) wide leftovers: 20–50mm ribbon of any length.

And now let's see how we can use these treasures!

Short leftovers

This bunch of ribbon leftovers is the largest in number. You can use them for:

1) Samples for dyeing
2) Eyelash technique
3) A flower centre: tie a knot in the middle of the ribbon length and bring the ribbon ends to the back.
4) A leaf or a flower petal: fold the ribbon in half across its length to work a loop.
5) Puffy petals
6) Supporting ribbon for Victoria Amazonica technique
7) Lazy ruche or Lazy jabot stitching
8) Creating a pompom
9) Keeping fine embroidery needles: make an area around your pincushion by attaching a small ribbon leftover using sewing pins. Now you can easily see where your fine needles are kept and you won't keep losing them among the huge chenilles!
10) Stitching a single-stitch leaf or bud
11) Working a petal in Wasp waist technique
12) Creating a colour card for your favourite colour combinations (see page 19)
13) Folding and gathering ribbon (as shown in the photograph below).
14) The Two-sided Janus technique (see page 41)
15) The Double tent technique for a petal or leaf
16) A petal for a knotted flower.

Long leftovers

1) If you are lucky enough to have just the right colour of the ribbon, use it for stitching in the ordinary way.
2) Lazy ruche or Lazy jabot stitching techniques as well as Ruche or Jabot gathering are possible.
3) Attach the ribbon to the fabric in a freeform manner to get a textured background, e.g. for a landscape.
4) Use the leftovers to practise new stitches and techniques. Then the ribbon colour does not matter so much.

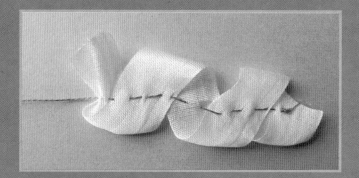

Wide leftovers

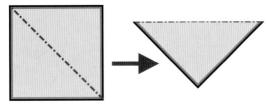 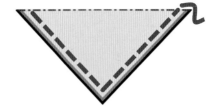

1) Head scarf method. Fold a square piece of wide ribbon in half along one of its diagonal lines (see the red dotted line) to form a triangle. Work Running stitch along both legs of the triangle (the blue dotted line). Gather the ribbon to get a nice flower petal.

2) Tent method (see page 38)

3) Hood technique (see page 61)

4) Coin-shaped rose method. Cut a circle or oval out of a piece of wide leftover ribbon. Finish its selvedge as marked by the yellow lines (A to B) in the diagram, using one strand of embroidery thread. Pull on the thread tightly to make a tiny mushroom shape, in the same way as you would cover a button in fabric. Attach the mushroom to the fabric, stitching through the stalk. Flatten the mushroom cap and embroider some French knots in the middle to mark the flower centre. You have made a lovely tiny rose!

5) Wide ribbon rose bud (page 39)

6) Cabbage leaf technique (page 38)

7) Half-cabbage leaf technique (page 39)

8) Belt technique (page 38)

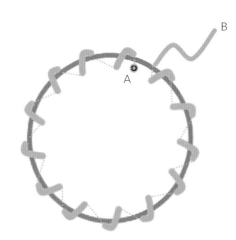

Coin-shaped rose method diagram.

Happy accidents

Your stitching mistakes can generate new ideas. 'Number fifteen on the right is in fact number eighteen!' wrote Helen Sergienko, a student of my silk ribbon embroidery workshop. She was right, this was my mistake. While drawing a template for a ribbon rose, I marked petal number 15 twice: once in the correct place, but then again where number 18 should be! We all make mistakes, but I hadn't realised what happy accidents can arise from them.

Once, late in the evening, a bit sleepy, I decided to grab some silk ribbon. In fact, late in the evening is an excellent time for insights and inspiration. Unfortunately the ribbon gathered somehow on its own threads – I don't know whether my fingernails had damaged it, or if it was a factory defect. Then I had an idea: why not use this as a 'Lazy' ruche technique instead of the laborious classical technique?

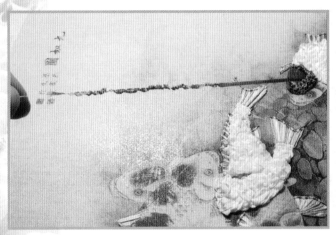

I often warn my students against coming through the ribbon with their needles on the back of the fabric. Well, perhaps someone should have warned me... I made the very same mistake, and it turned out to be right in the centre of a flower. To convert this mistake into a correctly shaped petal, I invented the Wasp waist technique, and since then I can't do without it!

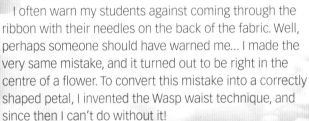

Having worked a line of Backstitch, I was about to bring the needle to the right side of the fabric, but the needle accidently caught the last stitch and it was difficult to unpick! Why not create a new stitch out of that? And so the Lazy tuning fork technique was added to my stitch treasury.

So before diagnosing a stitch as wrong or imperfect, have a closer look – it might be a new and original stitch!

OWLETS

I don't believe in the protective power of amulets or anything like that, but I am fond of symbols and tokens. Life is full of symbols: small items reminding us of something or somebody, or connecting us to a special place or event. A trifling thing may become a symbol, like a herbarium leaf, a bead or a tiny souvenir.

A couple years ago I was at the Masters' Golden Hands (now Craft, Business & Hobby) International Craft Show, held in my native city of Kiev. There are always many foreign participants and we usually make friends with them, which is one of my favourite things about the show. Once our American friends were leaving Kiev to return home. To say goodbye, they gave us a box of handmade chocolates. Inside the box there was a postcard with some kind words… and a strange stain right in the middle! 'Sorry about the stain,' our friend said. 'A tear-drop fell while I was writing those words.' What could I say? The tastiest chocolates were all gone in a day, but I have treasured that postcard ever since. That is how symbols work.

The owlet which is the basis for the first four projects is also an important symbol to me. Many years ago our online craft project was created and we called it Little Owl SmartCrafts, because owls are considered to be symbols of wisdom and education. We wanted our website to serve a wide educational function as we were planning to organize workshops, masterclasses, free online lessons and so on.

Later, a Japanese friend told us that the owl (*fukurou* or *fukuro* in Japanese) is a symbol of happiness in his country. This is because of the Japanese character for owl. As often happens for Japanese words, *fukuro* can be spelled in different ways, resulting in the same pronunciation but different meanings. Written with one character, it means 'owl', but written with two characters, it can also mean, 'no hardship or suffering.' Written with three characters, it can mean 'luck comes'. It was wonderful to discover this happy coincidence that we were unaware of when we chose the name for our business!

I would like to bring you luck and so I invite you to embroider an owlet of your own. There are four examples in this section of the book. Each owl is worked in a seasonal colour palette. You are welcome to follow my projects to the letter, or just use them as inspiration and make a quite different owl.

Owlet template

This template is used for all four owlet projects. The owlet is 6cm (2⅜in) from wingtip to wingtip.

Ideas for using the finished owlets

Needlebook

This is a flat case to keep your needles in, often arranged as a book with felted pages. This makes it safe to put them in your suitcase while travelling. Make two stiff pages for the front and back covers, as shown in the photographs, and attach pages of any soft material in between. You can easily find step-by-step instructions on how to create a needlebook online.

Tree decoration

Greetings card

Appliqué for an apron

Spring Owlet

The owlet size is 6 x 6cm (2⅜ x 2⅜in) and you can add stitching around it to fill as much space as you like.

Skill level: Beginner

Stitches used:

Straight stitch
Whipped straight stitch
Ribbon stitch
Rudbeckia stitch
Lazy daisy stitch
Spider web rose
French knots
Pistil stitch

Zigzag gathering
Victoria Amazonica technique
Lazy double ruche technique
Running stitch
Backstitch
Whipped running stitch
Whipped backstitch

YOU WILL NEED

Stranded cotton thread
Needles
• No. 18 chenille needle for 7mm ribbon; no. 24 chenille for 2mm and 4mm
• No. 10 straw or embroidery needle for thread embroidery.
• Piece of fabric with transferred template, see page 68, or find the kit for this design listed as K-049 'Fu-ku-ro Lucky Owls, Spring' on the author's website (see page 4)

2mm silk ribbon
• 1.2m (47¼in) black [1] (for pupils of owlet's eyes)
• 1.2m (47¼in) dark green (J021) [2] (for iris of owlet's eyes)
• 1.2m (47¼in) olive (S652) [3] (for body and bottom of the bridge of the nose)
• 1m (39½in) moss green (S658) [4] (for ears)
• 30cm (12in) quartz (S665) [5] (for middle of the bridge of the nose)

4mm silk ribbon
• 1m (39½in) olive (S652) [6] (for Straight stitches along body and outlining body from the bottom)
• 1m (39½in) variegated olive (V024) [7] (for body)
• 1.2m (47¼in) quartz (S665) [8] (for eyebrows)

7mm silk ribbon
• 1m (39½in) variegated sea foam green (V241) [9] (for wings)
• 80cm (31½in) yellow (S664) [10] (for feet)
• 30cm (12in) saffron yellow (J054) [11] (for beak)
• 30cm (12in) olive (S652) [12] (for top of the bridge of the nose)

70

Order of work

Read the Getting started chapter on page 8 before beginning. Here the picture of the owl template is joined with the image of the stitched owlet. It is very helpful to have this picture to hand while embroidering. The numbers in this template are referred to in the Instructions given below. Work symmetrical elements in pairs, using the same technique.

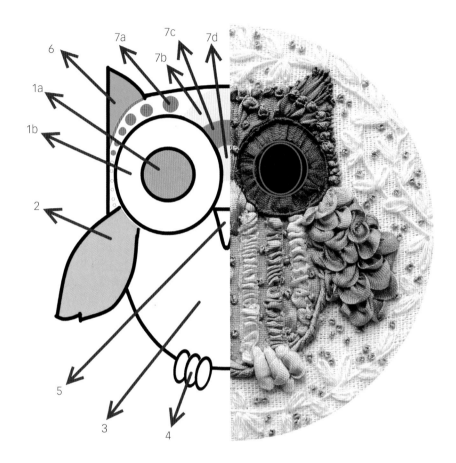

Eyes

Pupils

1a 2mm black ribbon [1]. Spider web rose. Work five stitches for a web in 2mm ribbon. Then using the same ribbon, start embroidering the rose. Note that it is used here for a pupil, not a rose, so twist your ribbon a little to get a smooth surface.

Irises

1b 2mm dark green ribbon [2]. Victoria Amazonica technique. Use two needles: the first for supporting ribbon (to fill in the rolls of the Ribbon stitches) and the second to work the Ribbon stitches. It doesn't matter where you start. While finishing the circle, go through the roll of the first Ribbon stitch with the first needle to connect the stitches.

TIP

Marking compass points around the pupil will help to make your stitches come out at the correct angle.

Wings

2 7mm variegated sea foam green [9] plus the toning pale green thread. Work festoons in Zigzag gathering technique. You will be more comfortable if you start from the tips of the wings and then proceed up to the shoulder. The rainbow-coloured arrows in the photograph (right) show the work order: each arrow stands for one row of gathering. Every row is supposed to cover half the width of the previous one. Note: do not fix the ribbon in the needle's eye, as it is not necessary to bring it to the back at the end of every row. While attaching the gathered ribbon to the fabric, take care to place the Stab stitches right where the gathering thread will go, as this helps to hide them. Work as many Zigzag stitches in each row as needed to cover the right amount of space in the wing. Making the final row a lighter colour will add charm to the owlet wings. Try to follow the pattern symmetrically while working the second wing.

Body

3 Work as follows:

Olive dotted stripes Firstly take 4mm olive ribbon [6] to work vertical Straight stitches, spacing them a little from each other. Then change to 2mm olive [3] to fix the Straight stitches with evenly spaced one-looped French knots.

Fluffy stripes These are placed in between the dotted stripes. Work them in 4mm variegated olive ribbon [7] using the Lazy double ruche technique. Attach the stripes to the fabric in toning thread. Now there is an option to outline the body from below in Twisted running stitch using 4mm olive ribbon [6].

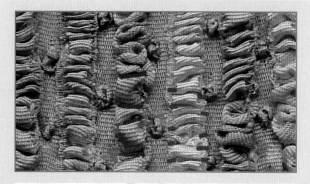

TIP

To make the job easier, work the Stab stitches in between the folds, as marked in red lines in the photo. (It will take much more time to work two rows of smaller Stab stitches – see the blue lines.)

Feet

4 7mm yellow ribbon [10] and Whipped straight stitch. For each foot, work three stitches, placing them close to each other.

Beak

5 7mm saffron ribbon [11]. Rudbeckia stitch. Work several stitches for the central part of the beak, one on top of the other to add relief. Then add one more stitch to the right and one to the left.

Ears

6 You probably know that an owl's ears are not made of the feathers! The feathers just mark the places on its head where the ears are. Use 2mm moss green ribbon [4]. One-wrap Pistil stitch. Place the stitches close to each other. The knots are supposed to outline the owlet contour.

Head

7 7a to 7d are the four zones of the owlet's head. Work the two similar zones (on the right and on the left) first before going on to the next zone. This will make it easier to place the stitches symmetrically.

Eyebrows

7a 4mm quartz ribbon [8]. One-wrap Pistil stitch for the upper part and French knots for the side part of the eyebrows.

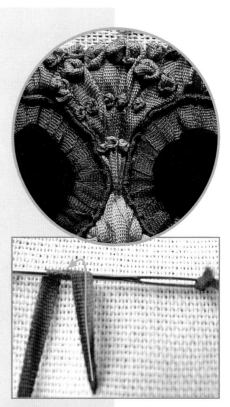

Bridge of nose, upper part

7b 7mm olive ribbon [12]. One-wrap Pistil stitch: work it, folding the ribbon in half lengthwise. This will make the ribbon half as wide, increasing the 3D effect of the stitch. To radiate the stitches evenly, firstly work the stitch in the centre, then one stitch to the right and another to the left of the first stitch. Now embroider two more stitches to the right and to the left of that group. Continue in this manner. Stitching this way really helps you to achieve a nice symmetrical shape.

Bridge of nose, middle part

7c 2mm quartz ribbon [5]. One-wrap Pistil stitch, radiating the stitches as shown in the photograph (top right).

Bridge of nose, lower part

7d 2mm olive ribbon [3]. One-wrap Pistil stitch. Work a fan made of very fine neat stitches. To make the job easier, twist the ribbon while stitching. If you are not happy with the shape of your Pistil stitches, consider the following options for improving its shape. There are two ways to start working this stitch. You can either go above the needle with your ribbon (green arrow in the photograph, above right), or go under the needle (orange arrows, right). Sometimes it influences the placement of the knot: whether it is above or under the stem of the Pistil stitch. Try both ways to see which one you like best. Observe the placement of the ribbon for the stem of Pistil stitches. It can either be flat or twisted. Both look nice, but you might find one or the other is the better option for different parts of the owlet head.

Background (optional)

8 Twisted backstitch, Lazy daisy stitch (both worked in two threads of pale yellow stranded cotton) and French knots in one thread of greyish-green stranded cotton. Draw a sketch of the spreading branches on a piece of paper or on the fabric using a fabric marker or watercolour pencil. Work Backstitch twigs along the lines. Add some Lazy daisy stitches for leaves and finish with groups of three or four French knot berries in between. You can also create a different design of your own!

Summer Owlet

The owlet is 6 x 6cm (2⅜ x 2⅜in) and you can add stitching around it to fill as much space as you like.

Skill level: Beginner

YOU WILL NEED

Stranded cotton thread
- White
- Mustard (toning with the ribbon)
- Cherry red (toning with the ribbon)
- Black (or size 15 seed beads)

Needles
- No. 18 chenille for 7mm and 13mm ribbon; no. 24 chenille for 2mm and 4mm ribbon and no. 26 chenille for thread embroidery

Piece of fabric with transferred template, see page 68, or find the kit for this design listed as K-051 'Fu-ku-ro Lucky Owls, Summer' on the author's website (see page 4)

2mm silk ribbon
- 1.2m (47¼in) black [1] (for pupils of owlet eyes)
- 30cm (12in) peach (S514) [2] (for iris of eyes, supporting ribbon)
- 2m (79in) bright white [3] (apron and daisy petals)
- 3m (3½yd) mustard (S660) [4] (head + feet)
- 1.5m (59in) saffron yellow (J054) [5] (daisy flower centres)
- 60cm (23½in) light green (J031) [6] (daisy leaves)
- 60cm (23½in) spring green (S647) [7] (daisy leaves)
- 1.5m (59in) variegated yellow (V039) [8] (daisy leaves)

4mm silk ribbon
- 1.5m (59in) peach (S514) [9] (for iris of owlet eyes, stitching ribbon)
- 1.2m (47¼in) yellow (S664) [10] (body and beak)
- 20cm (8in) saffron yellow (J054) [11] (beak)
- 1m (39½in) spring green (S647) [12] (body)
- 30cm (12in) bright white [13] (apron)

7mm silk ribbon
- 2m (79in) peach (S514) [14] (wings)
- 30cm (12in) cherry red (S527) [15] (crown)
- 30cm dark green (J021) [16] (rose leaves)
- 30cm (12in) hand-dyed bright purple (or scarlet S554) [17](crown)
- 1.5m (59in) hand-dyed burgundy (or cherry red, S527) [18](roses)

13mm silk ribbon
- 20cm (8in) natural white (or bright white) [19](apron)

Stitches used

Plume stitch

Ribbon stitch

Spider web rose

French knot

Twisted straight stitch; Rope technique

Victoria Amazonica technique

Tent technique

Star rose (with Colonial knot)

Colonial knot

Running stitch

Ruche gathering

Order of work

Read the Getting started chapter on page 8 before beginning. Here is the owl template joined together with the image of the stitched owlet. It is very helpful to have this picture to hand while embroidering. The numbers are referred to in the Instructions below. Work symmetrical elements in pairs, using the same technique.

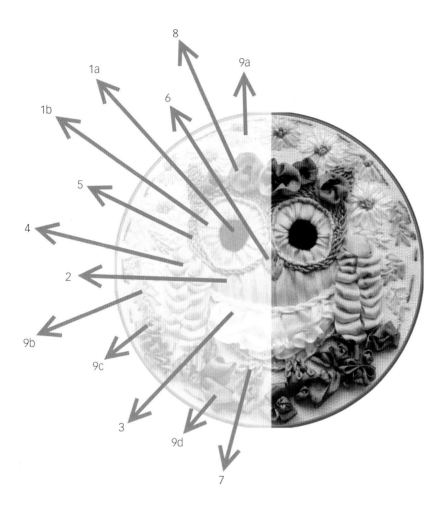

Eyes

Pupils

1a 2mm black silk ribbon [1]. Spider web rose. Work five stitches for a web in 2mm ribbon. Using the same ribbon, start embroidering the rose. Note that it is used here for a pupil, not a flower, so twist your ribbon a little to get a smooth surface.

Irises

1b 2mm and 4mm peach [2],[9]. Victoria Amazonica technique. Use two needles: the first for supporting ribbon (to fill in the rolls of the Ribbon stitches), and the second threaded with the ribbon to work Ribbon stitches. It doesn't matter where you start. While doing the last Ribbon stitch, go through the roll of the first Ribbon stitch with the supporting ribbon to join the stitches into a circle.

TIP

Marking compass points around the pupil will help to make your stitches come out at the correct angle.

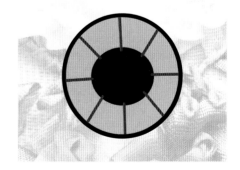

Body

2 4mm spring green [12] and yellow [10]. Mallet-shaped Ribbon stitch. Work vertical stitches, altering ribbon colour. It may be easier to work stitches in one colour first, leaving gaps in between and then filling the gaps with stitches of another colour. This time there is no need to fix the mallet shape of the ribbon. It is also possible to work the body using the Victoria Amazonica technique. Having stitched the stripes of the body described above, you will cover the apron image printed on the fabric, but this can't be helped.

Apron

3 2mm and 4mm bright white [3], [13]; 13mm natural white [19]. White stranded cotton thread. Ruche gathering and Rope technique from Twisted straight stitch. Gather a length of 13mm ribbon and attach it to the fabric for the apron. Then attach a ruche to the bottom part of the apron, working it in 4mm ribbon: fix the folds of 4mm ribbon along the bottom of the apron. Be sure not to stitch through the fabric this time – just through the 13mm ribbon. This will make the apron look more three-dimensional. The final detail: work a twisted rope using 2mm ribbon and fix it to the fabric along the waist.

Wings

4 7mm peach [14]. Plume stitch. Embroider two rows of Plume stitch for each wing, starting from the pointed bottom part of the wing and gradually moving to the top (shoulder) part.

Head

5 2mm mustard [4]. Toning stranded cotton thread. Rope technique from Twisted straight stitch. The head is all covered with 2mm ribbon 'ropes'. Place them along the eyebrows, trying to repeat the curved shape. Use one strand of toning stranded cotton thread to fix them, working tiny stitches. See the photograph, right: the pins are there to keep the the flower petals out of the way so as not to damage them while stitching the forehead and ears, as originally the flowers were created first. You will use a more intelligent sequence of stitching, following these instructions, so there will be no flowers when you work the head. Just don't forget to leave some space at the top free of 2mm ribbon ropes. This will save you time and ribbon and – last, but not least – it will prevent difficulties when you attach flowers.

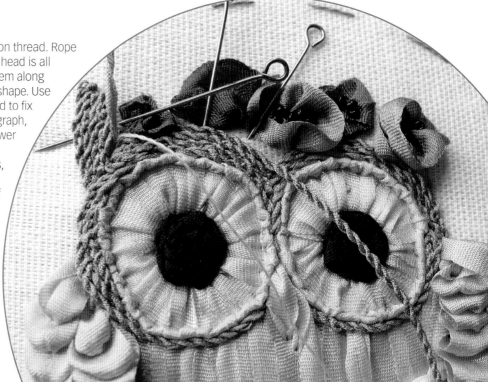

Beak

6 4mm yellow [10] and saffron yellow [11]. Mallet-shaped ribbon stitch. Create the bottom half of the beak first. Work one Ribbon stitch in saffron yellow, then a shorter one in yellow ribbon above this. Repeat for the top part of the beak, moving it just a little to the left compared to the bottom half.

Feet

7 2mm mustard [4]. Rope technique from Twisted straight stitch. Stitch three ropes for each foot (six in total). Make the middle rope of each foot a little bit longer than the sideones. Do not attach the ends of the ropes to the fabric for a three-dimensional look. Optional: if necessary, fix the bottom part of the ropes, anchoring them with a toning thread.

Crown

8 7mm cherry red [15] and hand-dyed bright purple [17]. Cherry red stranded cotton thread. Size 15 black seed beeds or black stranded cotton thread. Ruche gathering and French knots for thread embroidery. Work the petals first. Bring the ribbon to the right side of the fabric in the flower centre. Work about 2cm (¾in) of Ruche gathering. Pull on the thread and fold the gathered ribbon so that it forms a circle. Fix it using the same thread and bring the ribbon to the back of the fabric. Go to the right side in the middle of a second flower and repeat the same actions. Either add some black seed beads or work French knots using two strands of black stranded cotton thread to mark the flower centres.

Background

Daisies

9a 2mm bright white [3], saffron yellow [5], variegated yellow [8]. Ribbon stitch, French knots. Start working these flowers from their centres. For each centre, stitch four French knots in 2mm saffron yellow ribbon, placing them in a diamond formation. Now add Ribbon stitch petals in either bright white or variegated yellow ribbon. Vary the colours as you please.

Daisy leaves

9b 2mm spring green [7] and light green [6]. Ribbon stitch. For each leaf, work Ribbon stitches along one side of the leaf vein first, then go to the other side and finish the leaf. Work both parts of a leaf as a mirror image. Vary the shade of the greenery to add dimension to your embroidery.

Roses

9c 7mm hand-dyed burgundy [18]. Star rose. Place the roses as shown in the photographs. Here and there work some French knots for half-opened roses.

Rose leaves

9d 7mm dark green [16]. Tent technique petals. These might be replaced by the usual Ribbon stitches if you want them to lay flat on the fabric.

Autumn Owlet

The owlet is 6 x 6cm (2⅜ x 2⅜in) and you can add stitching around it to fill as much space as you like.

Skill level: Beginner

YOU WILL NEED

Thread and seed beads
- Variegated orange stranded cotton (background)
- Scarlet stranded cotton (to Stab stitch the heart)
- DMC pearl cotton (to outline heart)
- Gold metallic thread (background)
- MIYUKI Delica no.15/0 in two colours: DBS-379 and DBS-380 (to decorate the background)

Needles
- No. 18 chenille needle for 7mm ribbon; no. 20 chenille for 4mm ribbon, no. 24 chenille for 2mm ribbon
- No. 8 or 10 embroidery needle for thread embroidery

Piece of fabric with transferred template, see page 68, or find the kit for this design listed as K-050 'Fu-ku-ro Lucky Owls, Autumn' on the author's website (see page 4)

2mm silk ribbon
- 30cm (12in) black [1] (for pupils of owlet eyes)
- 30cm (12in) saffron yellow (J054) [2] (for iris of owlet eyes)

- 80cm (31½in) peach (S514) [3] (for side part of the head)

4mm silk ribbon
- 1m (39½in) black [4] (for pupils of owlet eyes)
- 1m (39½in) saffron yellow (J054) [5] (for iris of owlet eyes)
- 1m (39½in) moss green (S658) [6] (for wings)
- 1m (39½in) mustard (S660) [7] (for feet and eyebrows)
- 1.5m (59in) peach (S514) [8] (for eyebrows, forehead and bridge of nose)
- 2m (79in) olive (S652) [9] (for belly), 2m (79in) brown (S668) [10] (for belly)

7mm silk ribbon
- 30cm (12in) quartz (S665) [11] (for the beak)
- 1.3m (51¼in) scarlet (S554) [12] (for wings and ears)

13mm silk ribbon
- 30cm (12in) scarlet (S554) [13] (for the heart)

Stitches used

Straight stitch
Whipped straight stitch
Small bow stitch
Ribbon stitch
Spider web rose
French knots
Tuning fork stitch
Lazy tuning fork technique
Victoria Amazonica technique
Ribbon plus technique
Stem stitch
Whipped straight stitch

Order of work

Read the Getting started chapter on page 8 before beginning.

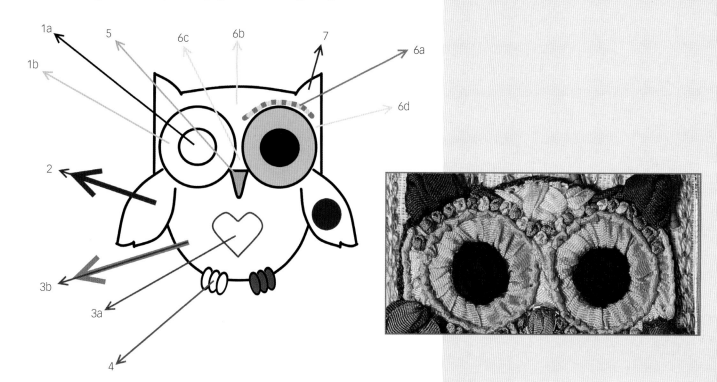

Work symmetrical elements in a similar way. There are two options: 1) stitch just the owlet itself onto a blank background or 2) add an embroidered background to this design. If you are going to work the background, it works better if you stitch this first.

Tuning fork stitch is worked in stranded cotton thread in this project. The rows in this stitch are alternated with rows of 15/0 seed bead twigs embroidered in between and framed by the lines of couched gold thread. The red and blue arrows in the photograph (right) show the changing direction of the Tuning fork stitch. The image left shows how to make the job easier, using Lazy tuning fork stitch. To work this technique, work long Couched straight stitches first, and then embroider a fork around each couching stitch. The photograph left shows the needle protruding through the fabric ready to work the first fork. Stitch the red fork first, then the orange one and so on. Do not go to the back of the fabric in the middle of a fork – just go under the couched stitch. Go to the back at the end of the first (red) fork and up at the beginning of the second (orange) one. Continue, keeping the same order.

Eyes

Pupils

1a 2mm and 4mm black silk ribbon [1], [4]. Spider web rose. Work five stitches for a web in 2mm ribbon. Using the same ribbon, start embroidering the rose. Note that the rose is for a pupil, not a flower, so twist your ribbon as you work to get a smooth surface. Change to 4mm for the outer rows of rose petals.

Irises

1b 2mm and 4mm saffron yellow ribbon [2], [5]. Victoria Amazonica technique. Use two needles. Thread a length of 2mm ribbon in one of them. This ribbon will be the supporting ribbon for this method of stitching. It will fill in the rolls of the Ribbon stitches. The second needle is threaded with the 4mm ribbon to work the Ribbon stitches. It does not matter where you start stitching the iris. Mark compass points around the pupil in soft HB pencil to show the correct direction for the Ribbon stitches (see right). While doing the last Ribbon stitch, go through the roll of the first Ribbon stitch with the supporting ribbon to join the stitches into a circle.

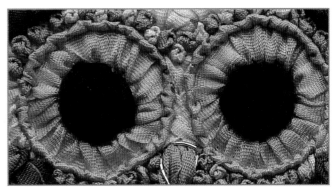

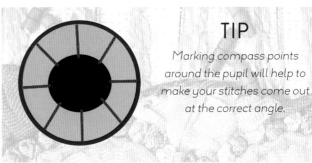

TIP

Marking compass points around the pupil will help to make your stitches come out at the correct angle.

Wings

The two-coloured 2 arrow in the Order of work diagram on page 79 indicates that two colours of ribbon are used for stitching: 7mm scarlet [12] and 4mm moss green [6]. Central ribbon stitch. Start from the tips of the wings and gradually go up. Thread two needles of the correct size with the two kinds of ribbon. There are two options for methods of stitching:

2a Use both needles simultaneously and work pairs of stitches: first do the scarlet base, then work the green top. Move to the next pair.

2b Work all the scarlet stitches first. Now take the moss-green ribbon and work all the green stitches on top of the scarlet. Make sure the green stitches are shorter than the scarlet stitches.

TIP

Make sure the wings are symmetrical. While embroidering the second wing, mirror the shape and direction of stitches of the first.

Body

Heart shape

3a 13mm scarlet ribbon [13]. Small bow stitch. The pink dot in the diagram (left) shows where the bow is fixed to the fabric). It is close to the bottom of the heart. The two bow loops are to be raised up and attached to the fabric in that position using toning thread. Thus the heart shape is created. Work a border round the heart with thick scarlet cotton thread in one row of Stem stitch.

Around the heart

3b 4mm olive [9] and brown [10] ribbon. One-wrap French knots. Place the rows of knots in your own way or follow the arrangement shown in the photograph.

Feet

4 4mm mustard ribbon [7]. Whipped straight stitch. Work three stitches of this kind for each foot (six stitches in total) using the photograph as a guide.

Beak

5 7mm quartz ribbon [11]. Ribbon plus technique. Work a short horizontal stitch at the top of the beak. This is a supporting stitch. Now work several Straight stitches, attaching them to the supporting stitch.

Head

Eyebrows

6a 4mm mustard [7] and peach [8] ribbon. One-wrap French knots. Starting from the bridge of the nose and going out in both directions will help create symmetrical eyebrows. Place the eyebrows close to the irises. Vary the ribbon colour as shown in the photograph or in your own way.

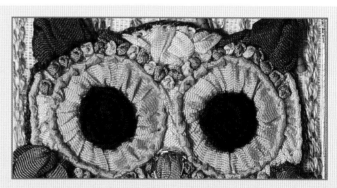

Forehead

6b 4mm peach ribbon [8]. Straight stitch. The stitches are crossed in the original design to get a more intricate texture. You are welcome to create your own interesting surface.

Bridge of nose

6c Stitch this in the same way, using the same ribbon [8] as for the forehead. Go under the iris to hide the ends of the stitches.

Sides of head

6d 2mm peach ribbon [3]. Victoria Amazonica technique.

Ears

7 An owl's real ears are holes in the skull hidden under its feathers. However, the two protruding bunches of feathers typical for some kinds of owl are always associated with ears! 7mm scarlet ribbon [12]. Ribbon plus technique. Work a supporting stitch at the base of each ear, and then follow the Ribbon plus instructions.

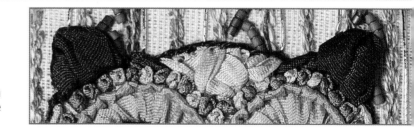

Winter Owlet

The owlet is 6 x 6cm (2⅜ x 2⅜in) and you can add stitching around it to fill as much space as you like.

Skill level: Beginner

YOU WILL NEED

Thread
- Pale lilac toning stranded cotton (for Zigzag gathering)
- DMC pearl cotton thread size. 8, colour 67 or similar

Needles
- No. 13 chenille needle for 32mm ribbon; no. 18 chenille for 7mm and 13mm ribbon; no. 24 chenille for 2mm and 4mm ribbon; no. 26 chenille for 2mm and thread embroidery

Piece of fabric with transferred template, see page 68, or find the kit for this design listed as K-052 'Fu-ku-ro Lucky Owls, Winter' on the author's website (see page 4)

2mm silk ribbon
- 50cm (20in) bright white [1] (pompom)
- 30cm (12in) black [2] (for pupils of owlet eyes)
- 30cm (12in) periwinkle (S579) [3] (for iris of owlet eyes)
- 2.2m (79½in) navy (S584) [4] (top part of the wing and hat edging)

4mm silk ribbon
- 1.5m (59in) bright white [5] (for hat edging)
- 1.2m (47¼in) black [6] (for pupils of owlet eyes)
- 2m (78¾in) periwinkle (S579) [7] (for iris of owlet eyes)
- 60cm (23⅝in) navy (S584) [8] (for wings)
- 2m (79in) deep periwinkle blue (S581) [9] (for head)
- 30cm (12in) sand yellow (S503) [10] (for feet)

7mm silk ribbon
- 30cm (12in) navy (S584) [11] (for wings)
- 30cm (12in) sand yellow (S503) [12] (for beak and feet)
- 1.2m (47¼in) variegated blue (V021) [13] (for body: select ribbon sections of a suitable hue)

13mm silk ribbon
- 30cm (12in) navy (S584) [14] (for wings)

32mm silk ribbon
- 10cm (4in) navy (S584) [15] (hat)

Stitches used:

Straight stitch	Pistil stitch
Ribbon stitch	Zigzag gathering
Double ribbon stitch	Backstitch
Reverse ribbon stitch	Bow on a fork
Raised ribbon stitch	Flood filling technique
Half-bow stitch	Victoria Amazonica
Spider web rose	technique
Lazy daisy stitch	

Order of work

Read the Getting started chapter on page 8 before beginning.

Eyes

Pupils

1a 2mm and 4mm black [2], [6]. Spider web rose. Work five stitches for a web in 2mm ribbon. Using the same ribbon, start embroidering the rose. Note that this rose is for a pupil, not a flower, so twist your ribbon a little to get a smooth surface.

Irises

1b 2mm and 4mm periwinkle [3], [7]. Victoria Amazonica technique. Use two needles: the first for the supporting ribbon (to fill in the rolls of the Ribbon stitches). Thread the second with the ribbon to work Ribbon stitches. It does not matter where you start. While doing the last Ribbon stitch, go through the roll of the first Ribbon stitch with the supporting ribbon to join the stitches into a circle.

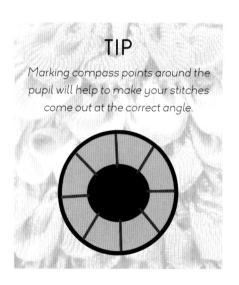

TIP

Marking compass points around the pupil will help to make your stitches come out at the correct angle.

Wings

2 2mm, 4mm, 7mm and 13mm navy [4], [8], [11], [14]. Ribbon stitch; Raised ribbon stitch. Work the wings simultaneously, matching them as you go to get a more symmetrical result. Start stitching on a wing tip, moving up to the shoulder. Work one or two pointed Ribbon stitches using 13mm ribbon for the tip itself, placing them flat on the fabric. This is the first row of feathers. Now change to 7mm ribbon and embroider the next row, half-covering the first one. Should you need to improve the stitch's appearance by going through a stitch in a previous row, make sure you press the previous stitch with your index finger to avoid damaging it. It is up to you to decide the number of stitches in each row – just work until you are happy with the wing shape.

After this, work the two rows of Ribbon stitches in 4mm ribbon. Work some of them with a short stem (see page 28). The top part of the wings is created by two rows of Raised ribbon stitch worked using 2mm silk ribbon. Place them as close to each other as possible, working them higher than all the others. This will make them look a bit ruffled.

Body

3 7mm variegated blue [13]. Zigzag gathering. Start from the bottom. Place the rows of gathered ribbon from one wing to the other, as shown in the image. Every row half-covers the previous one. Having finished gathering a row, attach it to the fabric using small stitches and toning thread. Select a good colour shade for the rows to your own taste.

Head

4 4mm deep periwinkle blue [9]. Backstitch. Work rows of Backstitch along the owlet eyes as shown. Working a right-hand row, then do the same for the left-hand side to keep the owlet symmetrical.

Beak

5 7mm sand yellow [12]. Straight stitch; Double ribbon stitch, Reverse ribbon stitch. Work the bottom half of the beak in Straight stitch. Now work a Reverse double ribbon stitch (see pages 26 and 27) for the top half of the beak and place it half-covering the bottom one.

TIP

Follow the photograph to avoid piercing your needle through the fabric at the end of the Straight stitch. Just fix it with a small couching stitch using either thread or ribbon (see the lilac ribbon in the photograph).

Feet

6 4mm and 7mm sand yellow [10], [12]. Lazy daisy stitch. Each foot has three claws. The central one is bigger than the side ones. Work the central one in 7mm ribbon and side ones in 4mm. Make sure the feet are symmetrical.

Hat with pompom

Hat

7a 2mm and 32mm navy [4], [15]. Flood filling technique; Backstitch. Attach one of the 32mm ribbon ends along the hat edge. Be sure the end is going to be hidden by the hat trim (see below). Twist the other ribbon end so that it makes this part of the hat narrower and bring it to the back of the fabric using a no. 13 chenille needle. Work a row of Backstitch around the hat using 2mm ribbon – in this way you will fix the hat and its folds in place.

Hat trim

7b 4mm bright white [5]. Half-bow stitch. Work a number of half-bows close to each other to make a fluffy surface and hide the edge of the 32mm navy ribbon work.

Pompom

7c 2mm bright white [1]. Bow on a fork technique. Work a tiny bow using this technique. A fork is too big for this tiny pompom, so fix four fine needles in a piece of cork (or a similar soft material) to imitate fork tines. Do not forget to increase the number of threadings (compared to what is shown in the technique description) to add more loops to your bow. Work ten to twelve compared to the five used for a classical bow. Having knotted the bow centre, bring the ribbon tails to the back in the centre of the pompom. Now look carefully to see if there are any gaps between the loops. If so, add one or two stitched loops (embroidering them in the ribbon tails) to create a continuous circle.

Background snowflakes

8 DMC cotton pearl size 8, colour no. 67. Pistil stitch. Work eight Pistil stitches radiating from the centre of each snowflake. Vary their length to add interest. Some of the Pistil stitches can be replaced by Straight stitches for variety.

SEASONAL FLOWERS

'Winter was doing exercises for so long that finally it got tired of it and BANG! – fell down. And spring came. Spring was doing exercises for so long, that finally it got tired of it and BANG! – fell down. And summer came. Summer was doing exercises for so long...'

By Gregory Popov, age 3

This is how my little son explained the phenomenon of the seasons. He certainly knew how to go on with activities till he dropped! I have never met a more active youngster! He moved so fast and so energetically that sometimes I thought he had the ability to be in several different places at once. I presume he had drawn upon his own experience to explain the seasons. Of course, nowadays all of us know what really causes seasons, don't we? It happens because of the Law of Beauty: to make more kinds of flowers blossom and to give us joy! Now we are going to enjoy stitching some of this beauty. Let's start with our spring floral favourites.

Lily of the Valley

Finished size: 15 x 20cm (6 x 8in)

Skill level: Beginner

YOU WILL NEED

Stranded cotton thread
- 50cm (20in) dark and mid-green
- 50cm (20in) yellow

Needles
- Nos 16, 20 and 26 chenille

Piece of linen/cotton fabric with transferred template, see opposite, or find the kit for this design listed as K-009 'Lilies of the Valley' on the author's website (see page 4)

2mm silk ribbon

- 1.2m (47¼in) spring green (S647)

4mm silk ribbon
- 1.5m white (use instead 7mm ribbon to stitch small petals and buds wherever you wish)

7mm silk ribbon
- 1.2m (47¼in) dark green (J021)
- 3m (9ft 10in) bright white

13mm silk ribbon
- 1.5m (59in) dark green (J021)
- 1.5m (59in) bright white

Stitches used:

Running stitch
Straight stitch
Whipped straight stitch
Stem stitch
Ribbon stitch
Side (right or left) ribbon stitches
Raised ribbon stitch
Lazy daisy stitch
Fly stitch
French knot
Hemisphere technique

Order of work

Read the Getting started chapter on page 8 before beginning.

Preparation

1 Transfer the template below onto the fabric. Draw lines for stems and for the central veins of the leaves. Mark dots for the centres of the flowers and flower buds, using HB pencil. Then start colouring the background using watercolour paints. Apply the correct shade of green to the space around the bouquet and the vase. Let this dry, then paint the three leaves marked with spring green lines in the template. Iron the fabric on the wrong side with a hot iron to fix the dried paints.

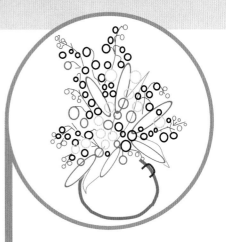

Template Key:

Leaves:

Spring green – painted leaves

Dark green – stitched leaves

Buds:

Green circles – stitched and dyed buds

Black circles – stitched buds, no dyeing needed

Flowers:

Blue circles – bell-shaped flowers

Yellow circles – flowers with yellow centres

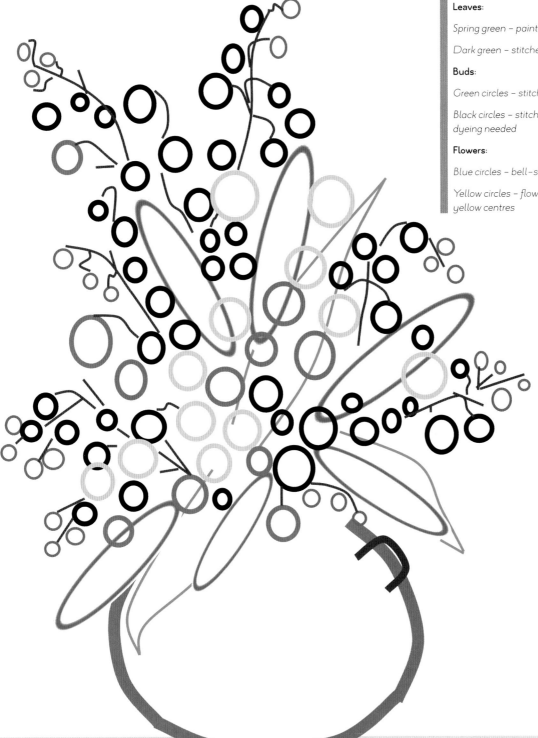

Leaves

2 Combining 7mm and 13mm dark green silk ribbon, embroider the six leaves marked in the template with dark green ovals (Straight stitches of different length) and fix the edges of the ribbon if necessary with one strand of dark green embroidery thread in very tiny Running stitches.

Buds

3 Use 7mm white ribbon for the buds marked with green circles and 13mm white ribbon for those marked with black circles. Firstly make a French knot with one, two or three wraps, depending on the size of the bud. Then cover the knot with one or more Straight stitches. Take care to start and finish stitches UNDER the knot, then the round shape of the bud will appear. If you start and finish the Straight stitches NEAR the knot, the bud will look like a rice grain, not a round lily of the valley bud. To finish, paint the buds marked with green circles using a light shade of green dye.

TIP

Use a second needle to keep the ribbon flat while working Straight stitches. Twisted ribbon will not work!

Bell-shaped flowers

There are two shades of white given for the 7mm ribbon: bright white and natural white. Use either or both. Using both shades in one design adds depth and gives a more three-dimensional effect to your work. Make some flowers smaller and others bigger.

Smaller flowers

4a Use 7mm white silk ribbon. Make a French knot first, then work three Straight or Ribbon stitches on top of the knot. You need to make these stitches longer (compared to the Straight stitches for the buds described above) to make the flower bell-shaped.

Bigger flowers

4b Combine 7mm and 13mm (½i) white ribbon. There is no need to start with French knots. Make two or three Ribbon stitches for the base, then work three more Ribbon stitches, trying to place them in between the previous row of stitches.

Flowers with yellow centres

Embroider these in a similar way to the bigger bell-shaped flowers. The only difference is that you place the upper petals high above the fabric. To do this, work Raised ribbon stitches instead of usual (classical) Central ribbon stitches. Work these in two steps.

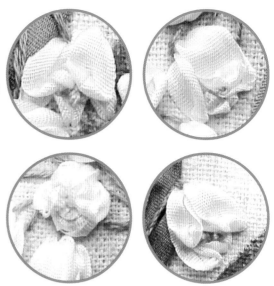

5a Push the needle through the ribbon as you usually do for a Ribbon stitch but do not go through the fabric. Simply let the ribbon go through itself, forming a nice loop.

5b Now go down to the back of the fabric, but be careful not to pull on the ribbon too tightly. Leave a small area of raised ribbon between the loop and the fabric so that the stitch is raised as if hanging above the embroidery.

You may also use Side (right and left) ribbon stitches for these flowers. Work some French knots in the middle of the flowers using two strands of yellow embroidery thread.

Vase

6 Outline the vase in Stem stitches with 2mm spring green ribbon. Work the vase handle in the same way.

Finishing touches

7 Embroider stems with two strands of green embroidery thread. Freely combine Stem stitch, Whipped straight stitch and Lazy daisy stitch. Leave some (Whipped straight stitch) twigs unattached to the fabric, allowing them to hang over it to enhance the three-dimensional effect. Mark very small twigs as shown in the grey circle (above). Use a tiny brush and watercolour paints. Some of the small twigs are embroidered in Straight stitches with green embroidery thread.

Your Day

When it's your birthday, it's certainly your day. It's also your day when something special happens for you, or when you are just in a splendid mood all day long, or you meet special people, or smile and get a smile back. This design is based on a watercolour by famous 19th century artist Paul de Longpré.

Finished size: 26 x 21cm (10¼ x 8¼in)

Skill level: Advanced

YOU WILL NEED

Stranded cotton thread
- 70cm (27½in) light green
- 30cm (12in) grey green
- 70cm (27½in) olive
- 20cm (8in) bright green
- 70cm (27½in) dark green
- 50cm (20in) light lilac
- 40cm (16in) lilac
- 70cm (27½in) dark lilac
- 1m (39½in) white or very pale yellow
- 70cm (27½in) pale yellow
- 50cm (20in) yellow
- 30cm (12in) saffron yellow

Needles
- No.s 16, 18, 20 and 24 chenille
- No. 10 embroidery

Piece of fabric with printed watercolour by flower artist Paul de Longpré (1855–1911), see page 197, or find the kit for this design listed as K-046 'Your Day' on the author's website (see page 4)

2mm silk ribbon
- 1.2m (47¼in) natural white [1] (strokes at the bottom of pansy petals)
- 1.5m (59in) lilac (S572) [2] (strokes at the bottom of pansy petals)
- 2.5m (98½in) plum (J084) [3] (strokes at the bottom of pansy petals)

4mm silk ribbon
- 1m (39½in) dark green (J021) [4] (stems)
- 1m 39½in) moss green (S658) [5] (leaves)
- 1.2m (47¼in) olive (S652) [6] (stems, calyces)

- 2.5m (98½in) dark olive (J171) [7] (stems, calyces)
- 1m (39½in) variegated olive (V024) [8] (stems, calyxes)

7mm silk ribbon
- 30cm (12in) yellow (S664) [9] (False bullion knot in the flower centres)
- 10cm (4in) mustard (S660) [10] (False bullion knot in the dark flower centre)
- 1.6m (63in) natural white [11] (False bullion knot in the flower centres)
- 2.5m (2¾yd) dark green (J021) [12] (leaves)
- 70cm (27½in) variegated yellow (V039) [13] (False bullion knot and a petal)
- 2.5m (2¾yd) variegated grape (V244) [14] (choose green sections for leaves and lilac for petals)

13mm silk ribbon
- 1.5m (59in) dark green (J021) [15] (leaves)
- 60cm (23½in) variegated yellow (V039) [16] (petals)
- 1.3m (51¼in) variegated olive (V024) [17] (leaves)
- 2.5m (2¾yd) variegated grape(V244) [18] (choose green sections for leaves and lilac for petals)

20mm silk ribbon
- 20cm (8in) dark green (J021) [19] (divide into four: use three parts for scallop-shaped leaves and one part for draping leaf, see Template)
- 40cm (16in) saffron yellow (J054) [20] (petals)
- 1m (39½in) light yellow (S655) [21]
- 60cm (23½in) hand-dyed dark lilac edge [22] (petals)
- 30cm (12in) hand-dyed dark lilac [23] (petals of the bottom pansy)

25mm silk ribbon
- 15cm (6in) peach (S514) [24] (petals)

Stitches used:

Straight stitch	Rudbeckia ribbon stitch	Ribbon plus technique	Buttonhole stitch
Arched straight stitch	Lazy daisy stitch	Long and short stitch	Folded straight or ribbon stitch
Looped straight stitch	Feather stitch	Open fishbone stitch	Twisted straight stitch
Ribbon stitch	Fly stitch	Tent technique	Open fishbone stitch
Raised ribbon stitch	French knot	Cabbage leaf technique	False bullion knot technique
Twisted ribbon stitch	Ruche gathering	Blanket stitch	Double tent technique

Order of work

Read the Getting started chapter
on page 8 before beginning. Make a
printed panel for this design (see the
Designs to transfer section, page 196).

The most fascinating thing about
this design for me is the gradual
fading of colours and shapes of the
peripheral flowers. It looks like a
photograph focused on the central
part of the composition, but it is a
watercolour. The famous 19th century
artist Paul de Longpré managed to do
this trick in painting long before the
art of photography became popular!
I aimed to show the same effect in
embroidery. I used thread embroidery
for the background flowers and leaves
and ribbon embroidery for the central
part of the bouquet. You can also leave

*The figures indicate the silk ribbon
numbers, as in the You will need
list (opposite).*

the background unstitched – be creative and do the embroidery as you like. It
seems to work more comfortably if you move from the peripheral elements to
the centre while stitching. Then you will be able to make the central flowers and
leaves stand out more from their surroundings. But this is the only restriction:
change the work order as you like for the rest of the composition. Most of the
images featured in the instructions show close-up details of the embroidery.
Every tiny thread is enlarged and this can make the silk ribbon look coarse. Don't
be fooled by this impression. If you have ever looked at a head of a butterfly
through a magnifying glass, you'll know it looks like a monster, not the delicate
creature it really is. The same thing happens to the ribbon.

Peripheral pansies, thread embroidery

1 Stranded cotton thread – check the colours of the image or select your own. Long and short stitch, Straight stitch, Blanket stitch. As mentioned, thread embroidery is used for this design to show flowers in the distance, whose shapes and colours are less distinct. This means you don't need to work them in Satin stitch or classical Long and short stitch, just work in broad strokes to create the petals. For instance, leave gaps in between the stitches and do not cover all the petal with embroidery – just work along its edge as shown in the stitching photographs below. Use different hues of the same colour for one petal to add depth to your embroidery. You can use either white silk thread or white stranded cotton thread. Both options will create a great look, although silk is better for the highlights.

The figures indicate the thread numbers, as in the You will need list on page 94.

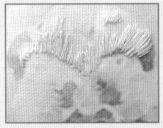 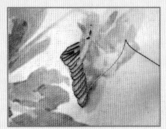 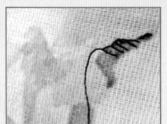 

   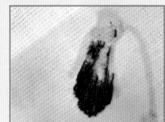

For calyces, use 4mm ribbon in different shades of green [6, 7, 8] and stitch either Straight or Ribbon stitches. Work several stitches one on top of the other to make the calices puffier.

Work Twisted straight stitch (or Twisted ribbon stitch if you are more comfortable with it) to embroider stems. The stitching will be more secure if you attach the long stems to the fabric, working Stab stitches in thread. The inset circle in the last photograph, right, shows a short extra stitch worked in ribbon to pre-fix the stem before fixing it with thread. This isn't essential, but it can be helpful.

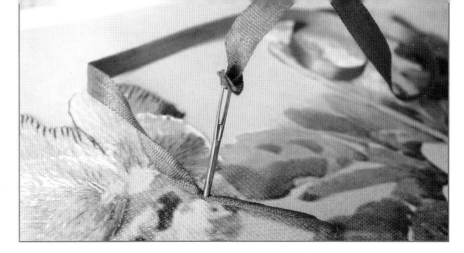

Stems

2 4mm ribbon of different shades of green [4, 6, 7, 8]. Twisted straight stitch (or Twisted ribbon stitch, as shown in the photograph). Just pierce the twisted ribbon before going to the back of the fabric. This will help to stabilize the stem before fixing its position with thread.

Top left pansy (placed sideways)

3 13mm variegated grape ribbon [18] (take sections of the shades as required), 13mm variegated yellow [16] and 20mm light yellow [21]. Cabbage leaf and Ribbon plus techniques. The photographs below show the process step by step. Firstly stitch the yellow petal, shading one of its edges in lilac thread (photo 1). Then stitch the puffy lilac petals using the Ribbon plus technique (photo 2). This technique will be very helpful for many of your future projects in ribbon embroidery. Work the supported stitches first, then go around them, stitching the petals.

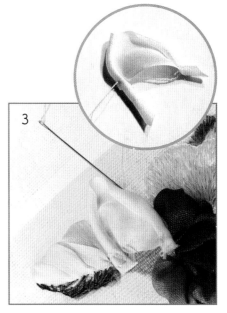

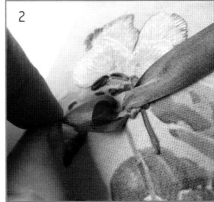

Photos 2–3 show how to finish working this flower using the Cabbage leaf technique for the pale yellow petals. The inset circle in step 3 shows the technique while the main photograph shows the placement of the two petals. To outline the petal edges, stitch them through with lilac stranded cotton thread (photo 4). The idea with this design was to create flowers in a rich colour palette without dyeing the petals. (Some people are not comfortable with dyeing, but they like the effect.) To achieve this, a lot of variegated and hand-dyed ribbon was used, as well as a variety of stranded cotton.

Ribbon leaf – Double tent technique

4 13mm variegated grape ribbon [18]. Double tent technique (see right). You will need about 10cm (4in) of ribbon to work the leaf. The ribbon is folded in half with each tail twisted into a short spiral (in fact, each tail is twisted twice). Then it is attached to the fabric.

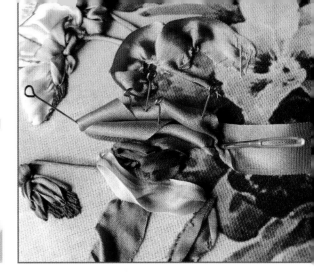

TIP

Pin the ribbon twists first to see if you are happy with the shape of the leaf. Then fix the twists with Stab stitches using a toning thread.

Leaves in thread embroidery – Open fishbone stitch

5 Stranded cotton thread in different shades of green. Work a Straight stitch about 1cm (⅜in) long, placing it along the central vein of the leaf, towards the tip. Work two X-shaped stitches around this. Follow this pattern until the embroidery of the whole leaf is finished.

The back of the work.

Leaves in thread embroidery – other stitches

6 Stranded cotton thread in different shades of green. Feather stitch, Fly stitch, Buttonhole stitch, Lazy daisy stitch.

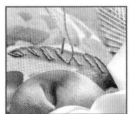

Feather stitch leaf.

The same leaf with some Straight stitches added in the gaps between the feather stitches. Use one tone darker thread for shading.

Fly stitch leaf. The stitches themselves fan out while the short fixing stitches at the base form a nice central vein for the leaf.

Buttonhole stitch with its rib going along the leaf edge. Leave bigger gaps between the stitches, of up to 4mm (⅛in). These will be filled with Straight stitches in a different shade of green or a contrasting thread.

Lazy daisy stitch leaf. Place the stitches along one half of the leaf first and then along the second half on the other side of the central vein.

Flowers in ribbon embroidery

7 13mm, 20mm and 25mm ribbon in solid colours and hand-dyed [16, 18, 20, 21, 22, 23, 24]. Use the image as a guide for colour changes. This is the most common way to work pansies. Pansies have five petals: two of them are in the top part of a flower (usually they are darker), and the other three are set at the sides and bottom. Follow this natural pattern to create lifelike pansies.

The ribbon flower will consist of two parts: a smaller one for the top two petals and a bigger one for the three bottom petals. The top part is V-shaped and the bottom part is U-shaped. For clarity, the images below show how it is worked both in silk ribbon and using strips of paper. The ribbon length featured is for 13mm ribbon. Use longer ribbon lengths when working with wider ribbon, for instance for 20mm ribbon, cut them 1–2cm (⅜–¾in) longer.

Cut about 7 to 8cm (2¾ to 3⅛in) for the upper petals and 11 to 12cm (4⅜ to 4¾in) for the bottom part. Cutting the ribbon at an angle is helpful for further work.

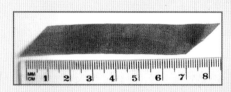

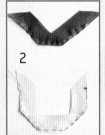

Fold each ribbon as shown (left): make one fold for shorter and two for longer ribbon pieces. Fix the folds using sewing pins. Work Running stitch along one of the ribbon selvages in toning thread – a contrasting thread is featured in the image (right) for clarity. The smaller the stitches you work, the better. Take care to leave some space at the ribbon ends unstitched. The line of Running stitches goes along the fold of the ribbon, stitching through the two layers.

Pull on the thread to get a nice ruche. Due to the folds, the ruche will appear divided into separate petals. Attach the petals around the flower centre, Stab stitching the ribbon with the toning thread. Bring the ribbon tails to the back and fix them underneath the petals. The flower centre should be clear of any ribbon going along the back of the fabric. Try to avoid making the empty central area of the flower too big. It seems to be more comfortable to attach the top part first and then the bottom part. Then you will be able to place the side petals either half-covering the top part of the flower or just sticking out sideways. Try to hide the Stab stitches in the ribbon creases.

Work French knots for the flower centre or use any method you like to finish your flower. In this case the pansies have further detailing and False bullion knot centres (see page 100).

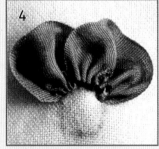

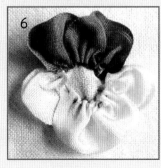

As already mentioned, the aim of this design was to avoid the need to dye the ribbon. Therefore I decided to work the markings around the flower centre, using 2mm silk ribbon (check the right colour shade or use a photograph as a guide). Work pointed Ribbon stitches (flat or on a stem), radiating from the centre. For the dark lilac pansy at the bottom, two shades of 2mm ribbon were used: first came the longer lines in white ribbon and then shorter lines in lilac in between.

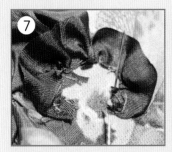   

Now for the final details: the three tiny rolls in the pansy centre. Again they were stitched, not painted. Just knot 7mm ribbon of the right colour in False bullion knot technique and attach to the fabric, protruding from the right side to the back of the fabric. As the two top rolls are of the same colour, the two knots were worked on the white ribbon. The ribbon tails were brought to the back and the three knots placed in the shape of a triangle. The diagram on the right shows the process of knot making. Work three-wrap knots to get bigger rolls. The resulting knot is supposed to have a rice-grain shape rather than being round like a ball.

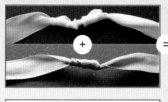 

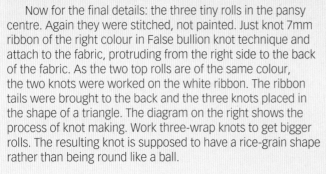

The last series of images shows one more way to work pansy petals, a kind of a freeform method. Shape the ribbon as you like, using sewing pins and then work Gathering and Stab stitches along the ribbon selvedge in the flower centre.

TIP

This method is sometimes useful while working flowers from hand-dyed silk ribbon if a definite ribbon shade is to be shown.

While finishing your pansy bouquet, keep to this simple rule: those flowers which come on top of their neighbours should be stitched last while those underneath should be embroidered first.

Leaves in ribbon embroidery

8 7mm and 13mm ribbon of different shades of green [12, 14, 15, 17, 18]. Assorted stitches.
This is a perfect chance to use your imagination! Just be careful that neighbouring leaves are of
a different colour shade and texture, as this will enrich your embroidery. The leaves in the centre
of the pansy bouquet are more dimensional than the peripheral ones.

The step-by-step images are for Rudbeckia ribbon stitch. The Ribbon stitch is worked on a
ribbon folded in two along its selvedges. Pull on the ribbon as tightly as you like.

  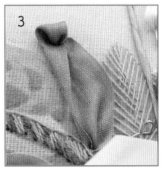 

The image on the far left shows the two leaves both worked in Straight stitches. Look how different they are! The one on top (with the white arrow showing the needle movement) consists of a number of Straight stitches placed at a different angle to the central vein. The leaf at the bottom consists of the two Straight stitches only – but they are worked in different shades of green ribbon and folded a little to show the texture. This is a kind of Ruche gathering. All the folds are fixed with thread, of course.

The Folded straight stitch featured in the images (right) is another option for a leaf. The ribbon is placed around the flower and fixed with sewing pins first, then attached to the fabric using matching thread.

One more option is shown here, step by step: scale-like leaves. Attach them in a pattern imitating fish scales. This is a variation of tent technique.

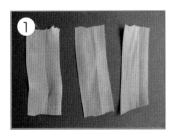 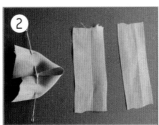 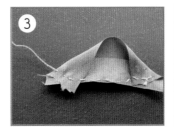  

From Olga's Garden

Some artistic souls have claimed they can smell the roses in this embroidery! This design is based on a watercolour by Catharina Klein (1861–1929).

Finished size: 27 x 19cm (10⅝ x 7½in)

Skill level: Advanced

YOU WILL NEED

Stranded cotton thread
- Green and white or pale pink thread (to fix the ribbon)

Needles
- Embroidery needle (for thread embroidery)
- Chenille needles: no. 13 (to make holes and support ribbon while dyeing); no.s 16, 18 and 20 (for ribbon embroidery); no. 10
- Straw needle for thread

Piece of fabric with printed panel for embroidery, see page 198, or find the kit for this design listed as K-038 'From Olga's Garden' on the author's website (see page 4)

Small piece of fabric for trapunto
Felting wool for trapunto
Aluminium foil

4mm silk ribbon
- 4m (13 ft 1½in) pale yellow (S655)
- 3m (3½yd) olive (S652)
- 3m (3½yd) crimson (S554)

7mm silk ribbon
- 10m (11yd) pale yellow (S655)
- 2m (78¾in) olive
- 1m (39½in) crimson

13mm silk ribbon
- 2m (79in) bright white
- 1.5m (59in) pale yellow (S655)
- 1m (39½in) pink (S550)

- 2m (79in) olive (S652)
- 1m (39½in) light green (J031)
- 1m (39½in) variegated pink and green ribbon (V237)

20mm silk ribbon
- 1m (39½in) bright white
- 30cm (12in) olive (S652)

25mm silk ribbon
- 1m (39½in) bright white

32mm silk ribbon
- 2m (79in) bright white
- 50cm (20in) pink (S550)
- 1m (39½in) crimson (S554)

50mm silk ribbon
- 1m (39½in) natural white or bright white

Order of work

Read the Getting started chapter on page 8 before beginning. Make a printed panel for this design (see the Designs to transfer section, page 196).

Study all the instructions before you start stitching. The work order is not fixed; it can easily be changed if you prefer (except where stated in the text).

Firstly I will give you an unusual method to create the texture of the basket.

The basket

Note that it seems to work best if you work the handle at the very end.

The back

1a Work Backstitch in 4mm pale yellow ribbon so that ribbon rows go ALONG the basket edge. Now embroider Raised stem stitch using 7mm pale yellow ribbon.

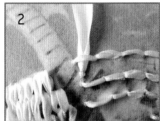
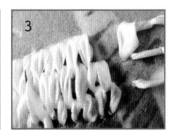

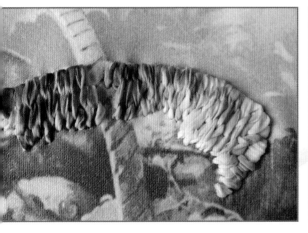
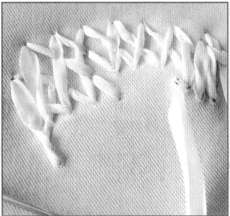

It is better to dye this part of the basket before the roses are embroidered, as this will prevent you from making spots on the petals. You can use special paints for this process, but the easiest way is to use watercolours. Use the photographs as a guide to dyeing. Apply some clean water to the stitches. Dye them according to the photographs or use your imagination. Use a hairdryer to speed up the drying process. Now add some more dark brown watercolour where necessary. The photograph above, right shows the back of the embroidery. Whatever you do in ribbon embroidery, the back always looks awful!

Stitches used

Arched straight stitch
Straight stitch
Whipped straight stitch
and a 'crescent' rose
Twisted straight stitch
Ribbon stitch
Arched ribbon stitch
Side (right or left) ribbon stitch
Folded ribbon stitch
Raised ribbon stitch
Ruche gathering
Backstitch
Whipped backstitch
Stem stitch
Running stitch
Blanket stitch
Wide ribbon rose buds
Chain stitch
Whipped chain stitch
Open chain stitch
Classical twisted rose
Raised stem stitch
Looped straight stitch
Whipped stem stitch
Tent technique
Cabbage leaf technique
Twisted ribbon stitch
Trapunto embroidery
False bullion knot

The front

1b The dotted red lines in photo 1 show the direction of Backstitch, worked along both basket sides. The lilac line shows the basket edge. Work a row of Backstitch along this edge as well. When finished, work Raised stem stitch, placing the rows in a semicircle (the light green lines in photo 2). Work these rows close together, leaving no gaps in between. (Ignore the finished basket handle and embroidered roses shown in both photographs. The images were chosen to show the basket, not the best work order!) Dyeing this part of the basket is similar to the process described above. The only difference is the radiating dark brown lines to imitate a real basket.

The two roses deep inside the basket and the one beside it

2 Use 32mm crimson ribbon (for roses 1 and 3) and pink ribbon (for rose 2). Those roses are all freeform. Fold the ribbon freely to create rose petals. Placing the ribbon in a V-shape and gathering along the cut ends works fine. Hide the ribbon ends under the rose petals. Do not forget to fix any ribbon folds with toning thread, hiding the thread stitches in between the ribbon folds. Rose 1: follow the pattern of fish scales or fir cones to place the petals (go here and there, folding the ribbon to work them). For the rose 1 centre: you may twist the ribbon a little. Dye if necessary, as described above. Use watercolour. It is better to add greenery at the end of the work. The photographs (right) show the details of the embroidery process. The dotted lines show the scale-like ribbon folds and the yellow arrows indicate ribbon loops. Using thread is very helpful, but it is also possible to pre-fix the ribbon petals with pins, to see if you are happy with the result.

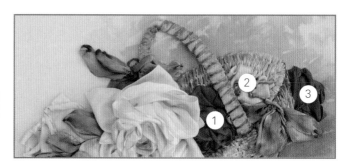

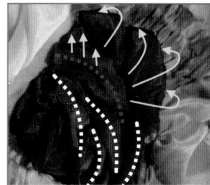

Freeform rose

3 Using 32mm white ribbon, work Classical twisted rose for the centre of the rose. Be careful not to make the centre too big. Attach it sideways to the fabric at the base of the rose, using white or light pink thread. Go on folding the petals, but now do this in an irregular order, however you like, using the photographs as a guide.

TIP

Pay attention to ribbon ends. It is not necessary to hide them under the petals as in the previous project. Attach them to the fabric as they are, stitching through the ribbon.

Dyeing the rose

Moisten the whole flower with clean water. Be careful not to apply too much water or some petals may become too heavy and change shape. When dyeing, remember it is always easier to add dye later than to take it away if you have used to much (use paper towels for this purpose). This is why it is usually recommended to use lighter colours first, then add darker shades if necessary. Remember that wet fabric or ribbon seems darker than it really is. Therefore sometimes embroidery masters use a hairdryer twice: once after the basic light shading, when you have the option to moisten the petals again. Then again after the darker colours are added. However, this is not always necessary and I did not use this method for this rose. Do this any time if you consider it to be helpful. Keep some parts of the rose close to their original white. Make the centre darker for a more natural look.

Regarding the colours: you can get pink either by mixing red and white and by adding water to red or scarlet dye. When using watercolours, I use both methods, trying out the shades on the paint palette.

TIP

Use a white tile as a palette as it is easy to remove extra paint from it after dyeing.

Four small buds

4 Use 13mm pink ribbon and variegated pink and green ribbon. A good start for all these buds is to make a Wide ribbon rosebud (see page 39). The only difference is that it is not always necessary to fill in the bud with a ribbon roll. You may use any material (e. g., cotton or felting wool to fill in the buds. If necessary, work some small stitches to prevent the tip of the bud from opening (see the red arrow in the photograph, below right).

Do not cut the ribbon ends. Use the extra ribbon to make freeform folds, showing the petals. Alternatively, you can place the ribbon around the bud and fold its ends, fixing them with thread. Add some dye in the appropriate shades.

One more way to shape the bud is to put in a ball made of felting wool (a felting needle is not needed – just twist some wool in your hands). Work a ball from silk ribbon, gathering it along both selvedges (see the Ruche gathering technique). Again, if any extra petals are needed, shape them from ribbon ends. Dye the tip of the bud, so that the bottom part remains green to imitate a real rosebud.

Finely, two Cabbage leaf petals placed around the Wide ribbon rosebud will create a nice tiny rose ready to blossom. All of them are charming.

Attaching ribbon ends is quite fiddly, as you need to make them invisible, hiding them under the buds. Use 13mm olive ribbon to embroider a flower cup to go over them.

Work stems using two kinds of ribbon: 4mm crimson and 7mm olive (creating the young stems from this year and last year's older ones), using Twisted or Whipped straight stitches. For the sepals use mallet-shaped Ribbon stitch. This will make the buds more dimensional.

  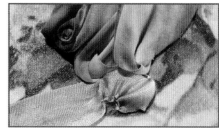

Small rose near basket

5 32mm and 50mm white and milk-white silk ribbon. A peculiarity of this rose is that its petals are all made from a single length of ribbon, not from separate petals. The only exception is changing the ribbon size. That is why I would recommend using the whole piece of ribbon to do it. Otherwise, it seems impossible to guess the exact length to cut. Start working it with Classical twisted rose, using 32mm white ribbon. Work just a few twists and – now the magic happens – fold it in half as if trying to reduce its height. Thus a charming mysterious rose centre is shaped. Attach its base to the fabric and surround with folds made of the same ribbon. Cut off.

Take 50mm silk ribbon and start working the outer petals. Go about 15cm (6in) from the ribbon end and fold it lengthwise so that one ribbon selvedge is higher than the other one (see the diagram, right). Work Ruche gathering along about 3cm (1¼in) of the ribbon length, going through BOTH ribbon halves (lilac dotted line in the diagram). Pull on the gathering thread, but not too tightly, and attach the gathered part of the ribbon UNDER the rose.

Instead of Ruche gathering, it is also possible to work Blanket stitch and then pull on the thread as you usually do to gather the ribbon. This will help you to make irregular, non-uniform creases, which is exactly what is required.

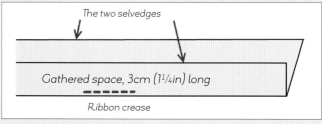

The two selvedges

Gathered space, 3cm (1¼in) long

Ribbon crease

What we have now is a sort of scarf going from under the rose, with two 'sleeves' (which is what I call these ribbon ends). One is about 15cm (6in) long and the other is as long as the rest of the ribbon length. Now one of the most creative parts of the work begins. Start to swaddle the rose centre, going around it with one sleeve first and then another. Fix the folds with pins first. Have a look at what you have got. If you are happy with the result, stitch the folds together, attaching them to the fabric. Any extra creases, upside-down ribbon or unusual folds which you would like to make and which look like rose petals are acceptable.

Petals of another rose, the biggest one, will be formed in a similar way. The few differences will be pointed out in the instructions.

Regarding the pinning and stitching process: sometimes ribbon 'obeys' and it is possible to create almost all the petals, pinning them to the fabric. Then you can stitch all of them and hey presto, the rose is ready. However, more often the ribbon is 'stubborn' and you need to fix it with thread having pinned a few creases (petals). Silk is silk – it has a life of its own. The main thing is not to be afraid of spoiling your embroidery.

The red arrow in photo 1 shows a tiny curve. This tiny space in the ribbon is stitched through, and then the thread goes through the fabric, but don't pull too tightly on the thread, so that the ribbon remains almost in its original place. The ribbon must not be attached too tightly to the fabric. If the ribbon were translucent, one might see a long looped stitch in thread between the ribbon and the fabric.

The blue arrow shows several creases, going ALONG the ribbon. The lilac arrow highlights the rolled ribbon end. This roll helps to move the outer petals aside, thus making the rose even more magnificent.

Don't forget to fold the ribbon over once or twice during this stitching process. When we started making petals around the centre of the rose, the ribbon selvedes were turned up and the petals looked thin. If you fold the ribbon, those selvages will be at the bottom, and the top part of the petal will look smooth and fluffy. Roses need petals of BOTH kinds for a more natural look.

Now make the petals which lie almost flat on the fabric. Use 20mm white silk ribbon. Photo 2 (below) shows the finished rose. The blue arrow indicates a petal formed by one ribbon loop (see Small bow stitch, page 24). The two red arrows show two outer petals. Fix the 20mm ribbon under the rose. No need to go to the back of the fabric – hide the cut ribbon ends under the petals. Make a loop, fix it with several small thread stitches and let the ribbon go around the rose, folding it a little while fixing with thread. Make one more loop and place it sideways on the fabric, as shown by the short pink arrow. Hide the ends and cut off.

Work one more loop for the petal shown by the long pink arrow. Make it as long as necessary to cover the space for that rose petal. While attaching it to the fabric, place the two halves of the ribbon separately to make the petal wide enough. Shape it so that it has a sharp tip. Work several tiny stitches along the ribbon selvage to attach the petal to the fabric. Hide the two ribbon ends of the loop under the rose.

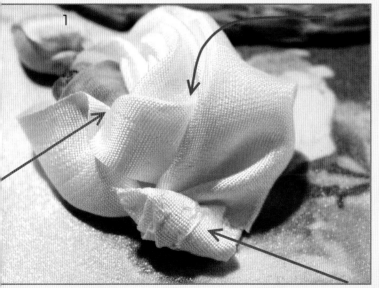

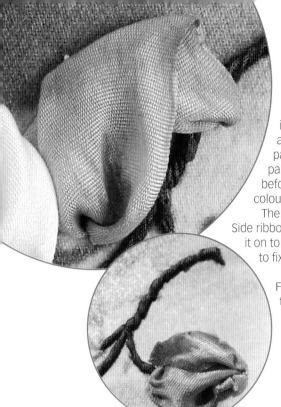

Stems and leaves

6 Use 4mm crimson ribbon for a rose stem. Work it in Twisted straight stitch and fix it in place with toning thread. Use watercolour to make the shaded side of the stem a little darker. Be careful when dyeing the stem: use a very fine brush to prevent the paint from colouring the fabric. Use a paper towel to protect the fabric or to remove paint spots if necessary. As the stem is rather thin, it is not necessary to moisten it before dyeing. Just use the smallest amount of water in your watercolour to prevent colour spots on the printed panel. Keep some parts of the stem undyed.

The leaf shown top left can be worked either in 7mm or 13mm olive ribbon, making two Side ribbon stitches facing each other. Note the tiny thread stitches shaping the leaf and fixing it on to the fabric. It is also recommended to make several small stitches at the tip of the leaf to fix and shape the Ribbon stitches.

The second leaf (inset, left) is worked in 13mm olive ribbon in Folded ribbon stitch. Fix the fold using toning thread as usual. Add some shades to the bottom and sides of the leaf.

Rosebud

7 First embroider the sepals under the rose bud. Work them in Ribbon stitches using 7mm olive ribbon. Now create the rosebud in 13mm pink ribbon using the Wide ribbon rosebud method. Use felting wool to stuff the shape. Note the fixing stitches in the photograph, right: the bud is attached to the fabric in two places, the bottom part and the tip.

Moisten the bud with clean water and add some pale pink watercolour to shade it. To complete the bud, work side sepals as described above. Work Straight stitches in 7mm olive ribbon across the bud to create the calyx and hide the ribbon ends. Dye them as you please.

Large rose at the back

8 The blue numbers 1 to 4 in the photograph indicate the petals worked in 20mm white ribbon. Any stitch can be used to make them. I did them in mallet-shaped Ribbon stitches. Dark lilac numbers 5, 6 and 7 mean the petals are worked in Cabbage leaf technique using 50mm white or milk-white ribbon. To take into consideration the fact that every embroiderer has her own 'handwriting' in ribbon embroidery, it should be mentioned that if your 50mm ribbon petals appear to be too big for this part of the design, change to 32mm white ribbon.

To dye the petals, moisten them; apply some pale pink shades, then some more dark pink at the bottom of the petals. Use a hairdryer – you know what for! Now add some more paint to the very edge of petal number 7. Use a fine paintbrush and only a little water in your pink watercolour.

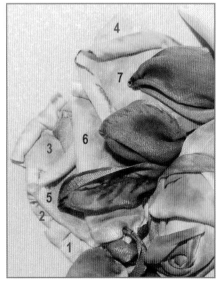

More stems and leaves

9 7mm, 13mm and 20mm olive ribbon and 13mm light green ribbon. Those leaves that lie flat across the fabric are all worked in either Straight stitch, Looped straight stitch or Ribbon stitch – the latter works especially well with 20mm ribbon). Place the looped stitches flat on the fabric and fix with thread. Fold some of them while fixing. Use the photographs below or your imagination for the selection of ribbon shades. Dye the leaves, leaving some undyed spots.

 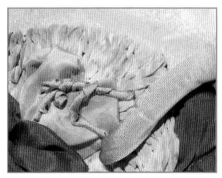 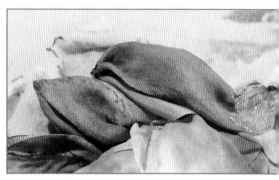

Protruding leaves are just a version of Tent technique leaves (page 38). The only difference is that the ribbon ends are placed one on top of the other. Note the way the ribbon is attached to the fabric: again there is no need to go to the back of the fabric. The ribbon ends will be hidden by the next leaves or petals. This works fine if you observe the correct work order. Mostly, the correct order means that you work the lower and peripheral elements first. Every time you start embroidering a part of the design, consider whether it will allow you to get to neighbouring parts. Dye the leaves as you like.

Stems are worked in 4mm and 7mm crimson ribbon in Twisted or Whipped straight stitches. The heavier the stem, the wider the ribbon you should use. Where a part of the stem protrudes above the fabric and is not attached to it, (see the photograph below), make a long Straight stitch, then whip it tightly and neatly. Crimson ribbon, dyed a little to a brownish shade, shows this year's young rose twigs. For the older twigs deep in the basket, use 7mm olive ribbon.

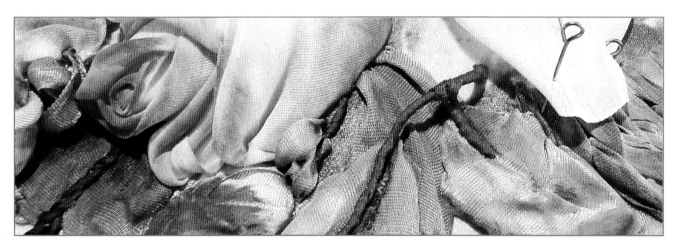

The largest sculptural rose

10 Work the separate petals which lie at the bottom first. Use 32mm white ribbon to make the first Cabbage leaf, but attach it to the fabric in an unusual way: place it SIDEWAYS. Look at the photograph (step 1): the ends of the ribbon are crossed (see the red dots which mark the ribbon ends). The tip of the Cabbage leaf is folded to make a even more interesting look. Attach it with thread as usual.

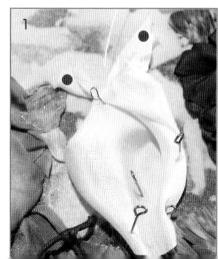

For the next petals use 25mm and 32mm white ribbon. Firstly fold the ribbon at an angle (step 2, right), fix the fold and place the petal flat on the fabric. The two black arrows show two pins which fix the folds temporarily. It is important to use pins for this design to avoid mistakes. The petal should cover all the space marked on the printed panel. Stitch it to the fabric if you are happy with what you have got.

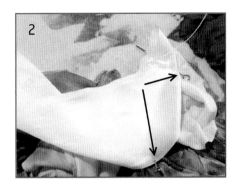

Attach two more lengths of 25mm white ribbon, gathering along their cut ends (the gathering will enable you to get more unusual petal shapes). Now is the time to get creative. Make the petals by folding and gathering ribbon lengths. Do not forget to use pins – they are really helpful – but be careful not to spoil the delicate ribbon structure. Be especially careful while stitching the finished petals with thread: the heads of the pins may get caught in the thread and the pins can then come out before you have stitched in this area. Do not pull on the thread too tightly or it may tighten the rose, spoiling its shape.

Change to 50mm ribbon. You can use either bright or natural (milk) white. As the flower is going to be dyed afterwards, it doesn't matter. I used natural white for clarity (see the photograph of the finished rose).

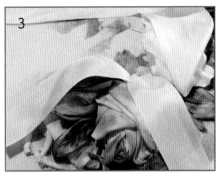

A Cabbage leaf petal (pinned to the fabric, step 4) is worked in 50mm natural white ribbon. You can tell the ribbon size in this project by the shade of white, as 32mm ribbon is bright white. The ribbon should not be cut off after completing this petal. It goes further to the other side of the rose and folds into a splendid second petal.

Using ribbon of different sizes – 32mm and 50mm – enables us to create more stuffed ribbon roses for a natural look. It also gives more opportunities to drape the ribbon.

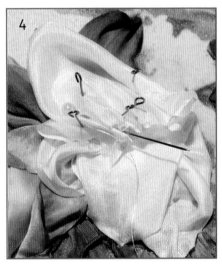

Now start making the middle part of the rose. The only rule is to keep it random! Zigzag folding, turning and twisting the ribbon all work really well. Do not forget to pin the folds first and then assess the overall look of the petals before you begin stitching.

Options for a rose centre

It is possible to start making the rose centre using the Classical twisted rose technique. Another beautiful starting point is to tie a knot in 50mm ribbon. Do not pull the ribbon too tightly, as usual: what we need is not a tight ball, but charming gentle folds. Do not try to place the knot on the very end of the ribbon. Go about 5cm (2in) along it and you will be able to use both ribbon ends to make extra petals, which looks lovely.

Another option when creating the rose centre is shown below. There is no single correct choice. The only essential thing is that the rose should be to your liking. Make a False bullion knot, leave it half-tightened and then fold it in half so that the smooth surface of the knot comes inside.

Alternative rose centre

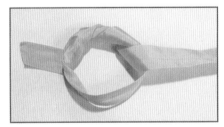 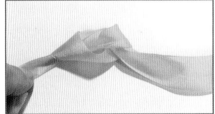 

1 Knot the ribbon as shown. The flat side of the knot is at the bottom.

2 Pull on the ribbon ends, but not too tightly. Then fold the knot in two.

3 Bring the ribbon ends to the back of the work or make folded petals out of them.

Be careful when fixing the folded petals with thread. This seems to be the most complicated phase of this project. It is not necessary to attach them very strongly. One or two small thread stitches are quite enough. However, the rose will probably need about twenty to thirty of these stitches in total. Work steadily and slowly. Otherwise, if you accidently pull out a pin, you can end up ruining the whole rose.

When finished, take a photograph of the white rose so you can remember it in this original state. The last step is dyeing the petals, and this is where the real magic happens. Moisten the petals with clean water. It is possible to do this either petal by petal or to make several neighbouring petals wet at a time. Apply some pale pink watercolour and enjoy watching the paint spread along the petal. Make sure you leave some parts undyed. Use a hairdryer.

The next phase of dyeing requires darker paint. Moisten smaller spots on the petals and apply watercolour to them. Dry them again. Dye the very centre of the rose to be the darkest shade. Use a just-damp brush to apply watercolour so that it does not spread too much around the petal. Be careful when using the hairdryer to dry petals made of wide silk ribbon. The hot air can help you to make a better shape from the wet petal, but it can also spoil a nicely shaped petal, making it flat and lifeless. To prevent this, do not come too close to your petals and blow round the petals from different directions. Congratulations, master embroiderers! The work on this rose is finished and the main part of the design is complete!

The handle

11 The basket handle is made using ordinary kitchen aluminium foil. This works as a filling to create relief and shape the handle. The steps below describe what I did, but you don't need to copy all of them precisely. If you think of any easier way to do the job, do not hesitate to use it! Fold a small foil rectangle in half and repeat several times until you get a foil strip. Fold and pin it at an angle as shown in step 2. Now whip this foil base using 13mm pale yellow ribbon. To make this easier, apply some double-sided tape at the end of the foil base. When finished, go to the back and pin the other end of the base to the fabric (step 3). Steps 4–6 show how to use the same ribbon to make an Open chain stitch in 7mm or 13mm pale yellow ribbon along the curved section of the handle. This is easier than folding the foil to create the curve. It would be impossible to use Chain stitch instead of the foil, as it would damage the crimson rose. Whip the Chain stitch using the same ribbon.

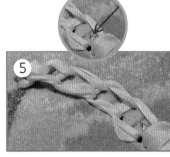

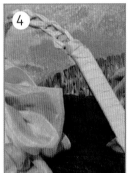

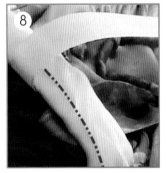
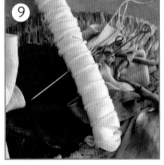

Steps 7, 8 and 9 show how to make the handle even more dimensional. This is not strongly recommended, just an option. Work a Twisted straight stitch using 7mm or 13mm pale yellow ribbon. Using this method will cause repeated whipping of the handle.

To add ribbed texture to the handle, use 4mm pale yellow ribbon, twist it tightly and whip the handle on top of the 7mm whipping. Leave gaps between the 4mm whipping and fix the ribbon, using toning thread.

Optional: work trapunto to add a 3D effect to the bottom of the basket. Look at the photograph (left). The blue lines show the trapunto area. Take a small piece of extra fabric. Place it flat on the back of the fabric and pin the two layers together. Be very careful while pinning: the holes made by pins should not be seen afterwards! Now work Backstitch along the outlined area. Turn the work to the back, take VERY SHARP scissors and cut a line along the middle of the attached fabric. Be careful not to cut the printed panel. Fill in the 'pocket' with felting wool or something similar such as cotton wool or leftover knitting yarn. It is very important to control the amount of filling. If you add too much, it will become too bulky and distort the embroidery. Stitch the cut closed using any thread or ribbon. I have used ribbon leftovers for clarity in the photograph (left, showing the back).

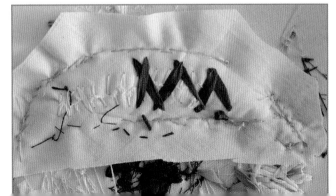

Dyeing the finished handle

Apply some light yellowish-beige to the whole handle except its left-hand edge (which mostly remains the original ribbon colour). If you would like the colour to spread all over the handle, moisten the handle with clean water first. Then you need a hairdryer. Apply some darker brown tone along the right-hand edge of the handle. Finally add some dark brown to the ribs (see the red arrows). As this colour is not expected to spread to the handle (only along the ribs), use a fine brush and don't add too much water to the brown watercolour.

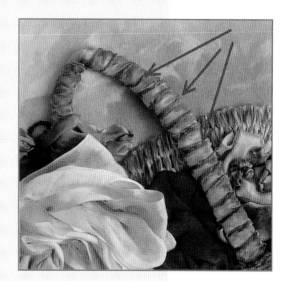

Finishing touches

12 Hold the finished embroidery away from you and give it a general look over. This is important because while stitching you are necessarily focusing on a small area only. Don't be a perfectionist. Everything handmade will inevitably have imperfections. If it looks good at arm's length, then it is good enough. You may find it necessary to add some details, fold a leaf or a petal and so on. This is a good time to do it. Don't play 'spot the difference' with the original photograph. From this point on, it is your own design with its own charm and beauty. Its main advantage is that it is different! It lives its own life and tells its own story. Your roses have their own scent and there is a piece of your soul in your embroidery. Frame it, take pictures of it and use it to decorate your room or to delight a friend with a charming handmade present. Be proud of it: a work like this deserves it. Happy stitching and enjoy ribbon embroidery again in your next fantastic project!

Meadow Posy

These wonderful daisies are based on a watercolour by German artist Catherine Klein (1861–1929). You may have seen a postcard of this design. Delve into history while stitching this embroidery!

Finished size: 20 x 13cm (8 x 5in)

Skill level: Beginner

YOU WILL NEED

Stranded cotton thread
- Any light colour to fix the ribbon tails on the back of the fabric

Needles
- Chenille needles no.s 18, 20 and 26

Piece of fabric with printed panel for embroidery, see page 199, or find the kit for this design listed as K-015 'Meadow Lady Guest' on the author's website (see page 4)

2mm silk ribbon
- 50cm (20in) light green (J031)
- 50cm (20in) yellow (S664)
- 1m (39½in) natural white
- 1m (39½in) bright white
- 1.5m (59in) olive (S652)
- 1.5m (59in) dark olive (J171)
- 1.5m (59in) light yellow (S655)
- 1.5m (59in) saffron yellow (J054)
- 2m (79in) moss green (S658)
- 3m (9ft 10in) mustard (S660)
- 3m (9ft 10in) brown (S668)

4mm silk ribbon
- 50cm (20in) light green (J031)
- 50cm (20in) moss green (S658)
- 50cm (20in) dark olive (J171)
- 1m (39½in) brown (S668)
- 1.5m (59in) olive (S652)
- 1.5m (59in) saffron yellow (J054)
- 2m (79in) bright white
- 3m (3½yd) natural white

7mm silk ribbon
- 30cm (12in) mustard (S660)
- 30m (12in) brown (S668)
- 30cm (12in) olive (S652)
- 2m (78¾in) saffron yellow (J054)
- 2m (78¾in) bright white
- 3m (9ft 10in) natural white

13mm silk ribbon
- 30cm (12in) dark olive (J171)
- 30cm (12in) olive (S652)

Stitches used:

Straight stitch
Arched straight stitch
Twisted straight stitch
Stem stitch
Ribbon stitch
Arched ribbon stitch

Folded ribbon stitch
Raised ribbon stitch
Rudbeckia ribbon stitch
French knot
Pistil stitch
Backstitch

Whipped stem stitch
Whipped backstitch
Running stitch
Whipped running stitch
Ribbon plus technique
Wasp waist technique

Order of work

Read the Getting started chapter on page 8 before beginning. Make a printed panel for this design (see the Designs to transfer section, page 196).

The instructions show how to stitch every element of the design, not the work order itself. As we are going to deal with a 3D bouquet, it is important to make the central flowers project outwards. Therefore, start with the outer flowers and gradually move towards the centre, following the numbers below.

Daisies 1–7

You can start stitching either by creating petals or embroidering the flower centre. It doesn't matter much this time. Doing the petals first will help you to hide the petal base inside the flower centre. On the other hand, stitching the centres first will help you to avoid distorting the petals. Just try both ways to see which one is more convenient for you!

Petals

2mm, 4mm and 7mm bright white and natural white ribbon. Straight stitch, Ribbon stitch, Folded ribbon stitch for flat petals and Raised ribbon stitch, Rudbeckia ribbon stitch, Ribbon plus technique and Wasp waist techniques for looped dimensional petals.

For flowers in the centre of the design, mostly 4mm ribbon is used. For flowers further out from the centre: some of the petals are created with 7mm ribbon as well. Use Rudbeckia ribbon stitch and Ribbon plus technique (for the latter you will also need 2mm ribbon to support the stitches). Note the back of the work (shown left). It looks a bit messy, but don't let it confuse you. There are very few places where ribbon is used to form long stitches, and this is important. Most of the ribbon is placed on the right side of the work. This helps you both to save ribbon and to create dimensional flowers.

Look at diagrams 1 and 2, right. Diagram 2 shows you how to save a lot of ribbon while stitching. The figures indicate the order of stitching. The dotted line shows ribbon on the back of the fabric. The yellow oval shape is a flower centre and the black oval is for the flower outlines. Following Diagram 1 has only one advantage: you can stitch all the petals in Ribbon stitch. Luckily the Diagram 2 stitching order doesn't cause problems because it is all right to make daisy petals a bit different. Let the odd petals (coming from the flower centre, 1 to 2 etc.) be Ribbon stitches with nicely curved pointed tips, and the even petals (3 to 4 etc.) be Straight stitches.

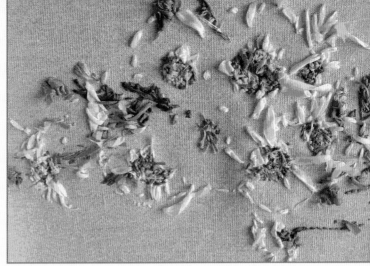

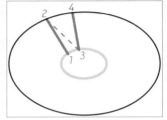

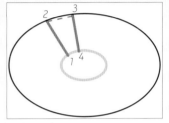

Diagram 1: The usual stitching.   Diagram 2: Saving ribbon

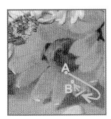

Another option is to make the even petals Ribbon stitches as well, but to place the curved tips near the flower centre. This will give your daisies an even a more natural look!

You could also use the Ribbon plus technique. Work supporting stitches first. Use 2mm ribbon to work Running stitches along the petal tips (use the images as a guide). Stitch either in bright white or natural white ribbon to match the colour of the petals, depending on whether the petal is shaded or stands out. Note the red arrows in the photograph (left): the stitches go either round the flower, forming a circle, or in a semicircle if a flower is placed sideways.

Change to 7mm ribbon to stitch the petals. Work a straight stitch from A to B (below), letting the ribbon go under the supporting stitch (see the green arrow). The ribbon will be folded a little at the tip of each petal. These folds recreate the tiny scallops at the edge of a daisy petal in nature.

If the supporting stitch turns out to be too wide for the ribbon size, work a second Straight stitch going under the same supporting stitch to hide it.

The idea of this design was to avoid dyeing silk ribbon after stitching. Therefore you will need two shades of white ribbon. In the photograph, no. 1 petals are worked in natural white and no. 2 petals are bright white. The green arrow indicates a supporting stitch. If you would like to add a touch of toning to flower petals, use watercolour and a very fine brush so that you do not add too much paint. You will find instructions for dyeing stitched flowers on pages 15 to 17.

These photographs show Raised ribbon stitches (right) and the Wasp waist technique (far right). The green arrows show the stitch 'stems' of the Raised ribbon stitches.

Flower centres

Use the photographs as a guide for ribbon colour changes. Stitches used: Straight stitch, French knot, Pistil stitch, Ribbon stitch. The usual way to work flower centres in ribbon embroidery is to stitch French knots. Working them with a narrower ribbon will produce smaller knots, while changing to a wider ribbon makes them bigger. You can also vary the number of wraps the ribbon makes round your needle to change the knot size. Alter the knot size to make your daisy centre look like a doughnut or a hemisphere – it is up to you; both shapes are natural.

Here are some more ideas for a natural look:

  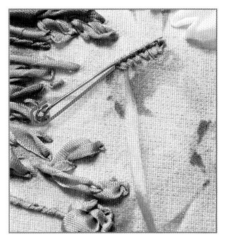

Work straight stitches radiating from the centre with 2mm or 4mm ribbon. Don't forget to use a fine chenille needle for stitching a flower centre to avoid distorting the petals around it.

You can also work Pistil stitches for a quicker filling of a daisy centre. Place them either radiating from the centre or crossed for more texture.

The red line indicates a sewing pin used to keep the mallet shape of Centre ribbon stitches while they are being embroidered. Work them around a daisy centre to outline it. A border like this should be worked first, before filling the centre.

TIP

While going round the centre, remove the pins from the stitches as you go, just keeping one inside the loop of the last one. Then go on stitching.

Flower cups

2mm ribbon of different shades of green. Raised ribbon stitch. A part of the flower cup is stitched in light green to show its lit side. Again, if such a contrast in ribbon colour looks unnatural to you, apply some watercolour to help blend the two.

Sideways daisies

2 These are marked A, B and C in the Order of work picture on page 115. Petals: 2mm and 4mm natural white and bright white ribbon. Straight stitch, Ribbon stitch, Arched ribbon stitch and Ribbon plus technique. Vary all these techniques as you choose. Note that for the petals protruding out of the flowers, you can just leave a ribbon tail cut at an angle. Stitch the centre of the daisy as described on page 117.

Buds

4mm and 7mm ribbon of different shades of green; 2mm moss green ribbon. Straight stitch, Ribbon stitch, French knots.

3a Stitch a French knot with 7mm ribbon, making one or two wraps.

3b Using the same ribbon, work one or two Straight stitches on top of the knot. Be sure to work these stitches across the stem.

3c Change to 4mm ribbon and work Ribbon stitches on top of the Straight stitches. These should go along the stem.

Stems

2mm, 4mm and 7mm green ribbon. Stem stitch, Whipped stem stitch, Whipped backstitch, Twisted straight stitch.

Twisted straight stitch with 7mm ribbon

4a The most popular way to work stems in ribbon embroidery is to embroider a Twisted straight stitch. As these stitches are going to be long, fix them with toning thread.

Stem stitch with 2mm and 4mm ribbon

4b This thread stitch works nicely for ribbon embroidery as well. Alter the ribbon colour and size for a 3D effect.

Whipped backstitch with 2mm ribbon

4c This is shown step by step. Make a line of Backstitch first, working fairly short stitches (photo 1). Then whip each stitch with the same ribbon (photo 2).

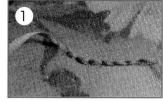

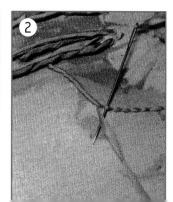

Leaves

5 2mm, 4mm and 7mm ribbon in different shades of green. Straight stitch, Ribbon stitch. Vary the ribbon colour as you please. Use 2mm ribbon to fix the weaving shape of the 7mm ribbon leaves in Straight stitches. Work some of the leaves in Ribbon stitches, going to the right and left from the central vein, using 2mm and 4mm ribbon.

The three–dimensional effect of the daisies. The red lines in the picture below right, show the areas worked using natural white silk ribbon. The other petals are done in bright white ribbon.

Autumn Basket

Golden flowers in an old basket... a perfect gift for an Autumn birthday.

Finished size: 27.5 x 20.5cm (10¾ x 8in)

Skill level: Advanced

YOU WILL NEED

Stranded cotton thread
- Dark green, yellow, saffron yellow, crimson

Needles
- Chenille needles no.s 13, 16, 18, 20, 24 and 26 for ribbon embroidery
- Embroidery needle no. 10

Piece of fabric with printed panel for embroidery, see p.200, or find the kit for this design listed as K-039 'Autumn's Birthday' on the author's website (see page 4)

2mm silk ribbon
- 7m (7¾yd) light yellow (S655)
- 9m (11yd) yellow (S664)
- 10m (32ft 9in) saffron yellow (J054)
- 3m (3½yd) peach (S514)
- 3m (3½yd) brown (S668)

- 3m (3½yd) black
- 1m (39½in) olive (S652)
- 1m (39½in) dark olive (J171)
- 4m (4½yd) dark green (J021)
- 1m (39½in) mustard (S660)
- 2m (79in) light green (J031)
- 2m (79in) variegated yellow (V039)

4mm silk ribbon
- 8m (8¾yd) light yellow (S655)
- 4m (4½yd) yellow (S664)
- 5m (5½yd) saffron yellow (J054)
- 3m (3½yd) peach (S514)
- 3m (3½yd) brown (S668)
- 3m (3½yd) black
- 1m (39½in) olive (S652)
- 3m (3½yd) dark olive (J171)
- 1m (39½in) dark green (J021)
- 1m (39½in) mustard (S660)
- 2m (79in) variegated yellow (V039)

7mm silk ribbon
- 5m (5½yd) light yellow (S655)
- 5m (5½yd) yellow (S664)
- 3m (3½yd) saffron yellow (J054)
- 1m (39½in) brown (S668)
- 1m (39½in) black
- 1m (39½in) dark olive (J171)
- 2m (79in) dark green (J021)
- 2m (79in) scarlet (S539)
- 2m (79in) variegated yellow (V039)

13mm silk ribbon
- 50cm (20in) olive (S652)
- 1m (39½in) dark olive (S658)
- 1m (39½in) dark green (J021)
- 2m (79in) scarlet (S539)

20mm silk ribbon
- 1m (39½in) dark green (J021)
- 10cm (4in) olive (S652)

32mm silk ribbon
- 50cm (20in) dark green (J021)

Order of work

Read the Getting started chapter on page 8 before beginning. Make a printed panel for this design (see the Designs to transfer section, page 196).

This wonderful arrangement has thirty-two flowers in it. This allows you to create your own botanical wonder with loving care thirty-two times over!

The photographs on this page show the flower arrangement as it develops from the printed fabric. Look at them from time to time to see the parts which become hidden while you are stitching.

Stitches used:

Straight stitch
Arched straight stitch
Looped straight stitch
Twisted straight stitch; Rope technique
Twirled ribbon rose
Ribbon stitch
Arched ribbon stitch
Twisted ribbon stitch
Side (right or left) ribbon stitch
Double ribbon stitch

Reverse ribbon stitch
Looped ribbon stitch
Half-bow stitch
Raised ribbon stitch
Rudbeckia ribbon stitch
Lazy daisy stitch
French knot
Weaving stitch
Chain stitch
Stem stitch

Whipped backstitch
Backstitch
Plume stitch
Tassel stitch
Wasp waist technique
Vertical line technique
Hood technique
Tent method
Whipstitch finishing
Flood filling technique

Working the design

• Start by working the furthest parts, gradually moving to the centre. This will make it easier to create the more dimensional central elements.

• Start stitching a flower or a leaf which comes underneath its neighbours. Then you will be able to place the protruding items in their correct positions.

• From time to time during the stitching process, put aside your needle and pick up a fine paintbrush. Having finished one circle of sunflower petals, dye them, and so on. This makes it easier to apply paint just to the right spots and prevents it from bleeding into the surrounding area. A fine brush works best as it takes less paint. It is much better to use only a little paint, as removing any excess is almost impossible. While dyeing, always have a hairdryer to hand. Take care so that the hot air does not damage the petal shape while the silk is wet. Do not move the hairdryer too close to the fabric. Use the eye of a no. 13 chenille needle to support bigger leaves and petals.

• The instructions give a detailed description of the most distinct elements of the design. Use them as a guide to work similar flowers. Change the stitching order as you prefer.

• The design consists of a basket and five types of flower. The shape of the flowers changes in a few places. Work these elements as you like.

• It takes a lot of silk ribbon to stitch this design, so saving ribbon is important where possible. For example, do not throw away 5cm (2in) ribbon leftovers. Use them to work several petals at the bottom of the flower. Don't forget that some of these stitches need immediate fixing with thread.

• Pay special attention to the beginning and end of every stitch. Again, some of them need to be fixed immediately to preserve their shape.

The basket

Vertical rows

1a Whipped backstitch. Work 5mm (¼in) stitches in 2mm light yellow ribbon, then whip the stitch line using 7mm light yellow. Dye the right side of each row in light brown or light beige watercolour.

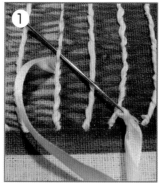
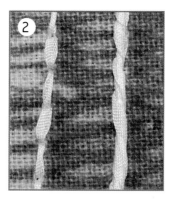
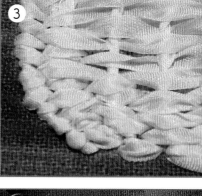

Horizontal rows

1b Weaving stitch. Work it mostly in 4mm light yellow, sometimes changing to 7mm to imitate the uneven weaving of a basket.

Dyeing.

1c Use brown and light beige watercolour to add shade to the right side of the weaving along each vertical line (see the photographs, right).

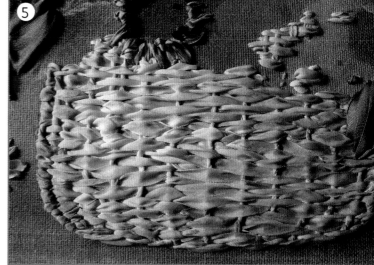

Handle

1d Stitch the two leaves under the basket handle first, using different shades of green. Then work two rows of Stem stitch along the handle contour in 7mm light yellow. Use the same ribbon to whip both stitches – be sure not to go through the fabric. Note that this whipping is not a finishing stitch. It is worked just to add volume. This is why you place the stitches perpendicular to the lines of the final whipping. The photograph shows the direction of the final whipping. This is worked in tightly twisted 2mm light yellow ribbon, placing the Straight stitches as close to each other as possible. This time the needle goes through the fabric. The stitches go diagonally.

TIP

When working these stitches, try not to make long stitches on the back: go up through the fabric on the side of the basket handle on which you have just come down.

Sunflowers with black centres

2 Work the petals in 4mm and 7mm ribbon, changing stitches as you desire. The petals of these flowers sit very close to each other. This may cause difficulties while stitching. To make things easier, every time you work a stitch, concentrate on two separate actions. First just bring your needle through the fabric, not worrying about the shape of the ribbon. When the needle and the ribbon have both come to the right side, shape the stitch as usual. Do not think of shaping until the needle comes through!

It is safer to fix the base of each petal with thread, working short Stab stitches (the white arrows in the inset photograph) to prevent distorting.

Working the petals first seems to make the embroidery process easier, particularly when you dye the petal base.

Try working a petal in two stitches, using a different shade of yellow for each stitch. This creates a wonderful effect (see the photo bottom right).

Making petals lie flat

Be sure to make the petals in the background of the flower lie flat on the fabric, while those on the foreground should be more dimensional. There is another way to do this in addition to the traditional ones described earlier. Bring the threaded needle up at the beginning of a stitch. Move 3–5cm (1¼–2in) beyond the probable end of the stitch and fold the ribbon in half at that point. Hold the fold firmly. Meanwhile bring the threaded needle to the back. Even twisted ribbon will go flat this way.

Saving ribbon

Try to save ribbon while stitching! Traditional ribbon stitching offers two ways for ribbon to come along the back of the work. These are shown right in diagrams A and B (the dotted orange lines show the ribbon coming along the back of the fabric). The advantage of option A is that it makes it possible to work all the petals in Ribbon stitches. The disadvantage is that you have to do rather long stitches on the back of the fabric. Diagram B shows a better way to save ribbon, with shorter stitches at the back of the fabric (thus saving the ribbon length). However, it is not possible to embroider all the petals in Ribbon stitches – you will have to work every even petal in Straight stitch.

I have developed a third way of stitching for this design (diagram C). The first stitch (brown arrow number 1) is for the first petal. Work it in Ribbon stitch and bring the needle to the back of your embroidery. The second stitch is shown by paler arrow number 2 in the diagram. It is important to start the stitch at the beginning of the arrow. Work a Straight stitch very close to the first one, in fact almost underneath it. This is not a stitch for a new, nice-looking petal, of course. I think of it as a filling stitch: we need to fill the flower with dozens of petals and some of them are going to be almost invisible, but their presence is important for a more natural look. Now repeat the first step. Follow the same pattern until you finish. This method produces the shortest stitches coming along the back of the fabric. You are welcome to use whichever method you wish.

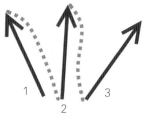

A. A good method: the usual stitching technique.

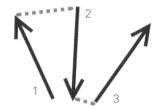

B. A better method, saving ribbon with small stitches at the back.

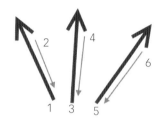

C. The best method, using the ribbon to make filler stitches.

Optional dyeing

You can dye the bases of some petals, applying a very pale shade of grey or brown watercolour. Be careful not to add too much paint! Always have paper napkins at hand to remove any excess colour.

Centres

Most of these centres are worked in French knots and Half-bow stitch. You can also place a Twirled ribbon rose here and there. Use 4mm and 2mm ribbon to stitch protruding or flat sections respectively. Use black ribbon to work the darkest parts of the centres. For lighter parts use peach and brown ribbon and dye it after the work is finished. A nice fresh effect will be achieved if you dye just the top parts of the French knots, leaving the bottoms undyed. Add less water to the paint to create this effect.

For a finishing touch, use four strands of stranded cotton thread to work some loops around the stitched centres. These suggest the stamens of the blossoming parts of the black flower centre. Cut some of the loops in half using sharp, fine-pointed scissors.

Flowers with petals dyed during stitching

For the petals, use 4mm ribbon in yellow and saffron yellow. Stitch half of the flower petals in each colour. Thus you get a flower with one half lighter and the other darker. Work some of the petals in Raised ribbon stitch for a natural look (see inset photo). Be sure to make the tips of these stitches pointed.

Prepare for dyeing by adding lots of water to watercolour paint to get a very pale shade of orange. Apply it to the base of every petal, leaving the tips undyed. It is easier to do this before the flower centre is stitched.

For the centres, use 2mm black ribbon to work French knots. Change to 7mm brown ribbon and stitch one-wrap French knots. Work a semicircle. Work Half-bow stitches around all the flower centres.

Use four strands of stranded cotton to work stamens as described on the previous page. Cut some of them in half using sharp fine-pointed scissors.

The faded sunflower

3 This flower has a black centre and no petals – just the sepals. Stitch the flower centre circle by circle: the outer circle in 2mm black ribbon with one-wrap French knots; the next circle, close to the first, in 7mm black with one-wrap French knots; then a circle of 4mm black with two-wrap French knots; and in the very centre, work Straight stitches in 2mm black. Lay the latter flat on the fabric, radiating from the flower centre.

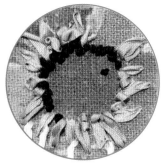

The sideways sunflower in the foreground

4 Half of petals of this flower lie flat on the fabric and the other half are lifted above it. Work the flat petals first. Choose from the advised selection of stitches whichever you want to use. Having finished, dye the petals using a very pale shade of grey first, leave them to dry, then add orange spots at the base of each petal.

Work the flower centre in French knots using black and brown ribbon. Now it is time for the lifted petals. Work them in Loop stitch, shaping as necessary to repeat the natural shape of the petals. Leave these petals undyed as they shade the flat petals beneath them but remain bright themselves.

The finishing touch is to embroider the sepals in either Arched ribbon stitch or Arched straight stitch.

Flat leaves

5 Use Flood filling technique to work some of the leaves and dye them with watercolour. Paint the fine veins where necessary.

Here are some more ideas on how to stitch the leaves:

• Straight, Ribbon and Reverse ribbon stitches worked in ribbons of different width. Sometimes a couple of Stab stitches in toning thread might be necessary to shape the leaves. Hide these in the ribbon folds or stitch them near the tip or base of the leaf to make them invisible.

• Limit the colours. Mostly it is dark green; just a couple of the leaves are worked in different shades of olive. It is important not to work the greenery of this bouquet in too many colours because the flowers should stand out.

• Also limit the colours used for dyeing parts of some leaves. Exercise moderation! And do not forget about the leaf veins which appear here and there.

• One more trick is to fix the selvedge of the wide ribbon used for the leaf in Plume stitch. Work the stitch, laying it flat around the leaf contour. Use 2mm ribbon for the Plume stitch. Use the photographs as a guide for colour changes.

Teddy bear sunflowers

6 These have no black centre. Mostly 2mm ribbon is used here, with a few stitches worked in 4mm. Think about the differences between a sunflower's and a dandelion's shape. Of course they are different sizes and this shows in nature but when you see a stitched flower, it is not always easy to guess the scale. Look at photographs of dandelions: their outer petals often seem far longer than the others. Then consider the centre. A dandelion in half-bloom often has a narrow space inside it where the petals stay very close together. The Teddy bear sunflower shape is different. All the petals seem to be the same length and the middle is a remnant of the usual black sunflower centre. It is flat and greenish. All this means that it is important to observe the length of the outer petals compared to the others.

Work the first layer of petals (coming around the flower contour) in 2mm ribbon, using 4mm at random to add interest. Dye their bases, but do not make them too bright. Then come to the next (inner) circle of flower petals and work them in between the petals of the first layer. When coming closer to the flower centre, lift the petals. For example the first circle of petals is worked in Ribbon stitch, the next two are Arched ribbon stitches, the next are Raised ribbon stitches etc. Most of the Raised ribbon stitches are pointed.

In the very centre, work the petals in the Rope technique (of Twisted straight stitch) and Tassel stitch. Be careful not to destroy the finished stitches while creating new ones. Use all shades of yellow ribbon and different stitches to work the Teddy bear sunflowers. The Wasp waist technique also works nicely.

Dyeing the Teddy petals is a bit different from the usual dyeing. Having finished one circle of petals, apply the paint to their bases.

Order of work

Work one circle of flat petals. Each subsequent circle is raised a little above the previous one. Dye as desired.

Work one more circle of lifted petals, each stitch starting almost from the flower centre.

Now work similar petals, but shorter. Dye the bases in a darker shade, say orange to brown.

Rudbeckia

7 These have a dark orange stripe on the petals. Petals: 7mm ribbon, colour shades as in the photograph. Ribbon and Twisted ribbon stitches.

Flower centre: French knots in 4mm and 7mm brown ribbon. Dye as necessary. The knots in the middle are to be dyed completely, but for those around them, just apply some dye on the top. Leaving their sides light helps create more vivid flowers.

Dyeing the petals: it is important not to add too much water to the watercolour, so that the paint does not bleed. Use a hairdryer to speed up drying.

Doronicum Orientale

8 These are the smaller yellow flowers. For the petals use 4mm yellow and saffron yellow ribbon. Work them in Straight and Ribbon stitches. Add a few petals in 4mm light yellow ribbon to show highlights. Having finished the petals, apply some very pale grey watercolour to fade them. For some flowers, work the second layer of petals. Embroider the flower centres in French knots using 2mm brown ribbon. Add some knots in 4mm ribbon to make the centres come forwards.

Nasturtiums

9 These are the red flowers. 13mm scarlet ribbon for the bigger flowers and 7mm for the smaller ones. Apply some very pale grey watercolour to some of the petals to fade them. The way to stitch nasturtiums is perfectly explained in ribbon embroidery books by Ann Cox. Each petal is a Looped ribbon stitch. Work five petals for each flower and fix each of them in Stab stitches using toning thread. For stamens make Tassel stitches in the flower centre using a mix of orange and burgundy threads. For some of the petals you can also apply the Vertical line technique: work a Looped ribbon stitch in 7mm ribbon, then add a Lazy daisy stitch around it. For a better appearance, be sure not to work a securing stitch over the loop.

The three-dimensional leaves in the centre

10 Use any wide dark green ribbon: 20mm or 32mm for the Hood technique. Create leaves of different sizes as in the image. Start with those in the background.

There is an option to decorate the middle part of the leaf rosette by working rope-shaped Twisted straight stitches in 2mm dark green.

TIP

The work will be far easier if you do not bring the ribbon tails to the back of the embroidery. Hide them under the neighbouring leaves.

Finishing touches

11 Have a look at your artwork, judging it in general: maybe a tiny detail has been missed or a petal or leaf needs shaping. Perhaps you would like to add some more stamens or other details. It's your work now so do as you please!

Sunny Road

This design is in the style of a traditional Chinese guohua painting. It makes a nice piece of appliqué, shown here on a handmade bag. Make sure all the ribbon tails are fixed properly on the back of the fabric.

Finished size: 20 x 20cm (8 x 8in)

Skill level: Intermediate

YOU WILL NEED

Stranded cotton thread
- Three shades of olive, dark grey

DMC pearl cotton thread size 8

Needles
- Chenille needles no. 18 for 7mm and 13mm ribbon; no. 20 for 4mm and 7mm ribbon; no. 24 for 2mm ribbon and thread

Piece of fabric with printed panel for embroidery, see page 201 or find the kit for this design listed as K-032 'Road Under the Sun' on the author's website (see page 4)

2mm silk ribbon
- 3m (3½yd) saffron yellow (J054) (petals)
- 3m (3½yd) pale yellow (S655) (petals)
- 4m (4½yd) black (centres)
- 4m (4½yd) dark olive (J171) (leaf scallops)
- 7m (7¾yd) olive (S652) (leaf scallops)
- 5m (5½yd) yellow (S664) (petals)
- 6m (6¾yd)moss green (S658) (leaf scallops and needlelace)
- 10m (11yd) quartz (S665) (needlelace)
- 30cm (12in) variegated olive (V024) (leaf scallops)
- 3m (3½yd) variegated yellow (V039) (petals)

4mm silk ribbon
- 1m (39½in) olive (S652) (background leaves)
- 1m (39½in) saffron yellow (J054) (petals)
- 3m (3½yd) pale yellow (S655) (petals)
- 5m (5½yd) yellow (S664) (petals)
- 30cm (12in) variegated olive (V024) (background leaves)
- 3m (3½yd) variegated yellow (V039) (petals)

7mm silk ribbon
- 1m (39½in) light green (J031) (leaves)
- 1m (39½in) quartz (S665) (leaves)
- 2m (79in) olive (S652) (leaves)
- 2m (79in) dark olive (J171) (leaves)
- 2m (79in) moss green (S658) (leaves)
- 2m (79in) saffron yellow (J054) (centres and buds)
- 3m (3½yd) yellow (S664) (centres and buds)
- 50cm (20in) variegated olive (V024) (leaves)
- 1m (39½in) variegated sea green (V241) (background leaves)

13mm silk ribbon
- 50cm (20in) dark olive (J171) (foreground leaves)
- 1m (39½in) olive (S652) (foreground leaves)
- 1m (39½in) moss green (S658) (foreground leaves)
- 1m (39½in) quartz (S665) (foreground leaves)

Stitches used:

Straight stitch
Raised ribbon stitch
French knot
Couched straight stitch
Twisted straight stitch
Fly stitch
Ribbon stitch
Eye-looped stitch
Whipstitch finishing
Woven circle filling needlelace
Arched straight stitch
Looped straight stitch
Hemisphere technique

Order of work

Read the Getting started chapter on page 8 before beginning. Make a printed panel for this design (see the Designs to transfer section, page 196). The work order for this design is not fixed. You are welcome to change it as you like.

Flowers

1 2mm and 4mm pale yellow, yellow, saffron yellow and variegated yellow ribbon; 2mm black ribbon. Central ribbon stitch, Straight stitch, Arched straight stitch, Raised ribbon stitch, Eye-looped stitch, French knot. The sequence of stitching for every flower consists of three steps:

a Work 'sun rays' around the flower centre, laying the stitches flat.

b Work some 3D petals. Most of them are shorter than the others.

c Embroider an Eye-looped stitch in the centre. The red arrows in the photograph (far right) show Raised ribbon stitches; the lilac arrow indicates several loops stitched around the flower centre (optional).

Leaves

2 2mm, 7mm and 13mm ribbon in different shades of green, including some variegated sea-green. Pearl cotton or similar thread in different shades of green. Ribbon stitch, Straight stitch, Twisted straight stitch, Fly stitch, Whipstitch finishing. All the leaves are worked following the same pattern: stitch a Ribbon stitch or a Straight stitch along all the leaf, and then add some tiny scales along the leaf edge in Straight stitch or using Whipstitch finishing.

Optional for bigger leaves only: work a central vein in Twisted straight stitch using 2mm ribbon. Add more veins and vary the shade of green as you please. Bear in mind that you might run out of your favourite ribbon shades if you use them too much. Should this happen, be creative and use another ribbon instead.

Some of the leaves are stitched in thread: pearl cotton DMC and similar. Work just a couple of the leaves in this way to add some texture to the design. Start stitching with a Straight stitch (the orange line in the diagram, right). Now surround the Straight stitch with a group of Fly stitches (the one marked in dark blue lines comes first). Place all the stitches close to each other. Keep working them until all the leaf surface is covered.

Flower buds

3 7mm yellow and saffron yellow ribbon. French knots, Straight stitch, Hemisphere technique.

Woven circle filling needlelace

4 2mm moss green and quartz silk ribbon. Pearl cotton or similar thread of dark shades of grey. Couched straight stitch, French knots.

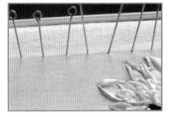

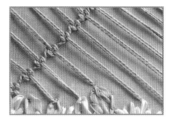

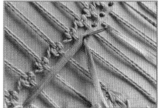

a Mark the panel edge approx. every 5mm (¼in). Sewing pins or HB pencil are helpful. Do not use water soluble marker or the printed panel might be damaged while dissolving the marks.

b Work supporting threads. Make them double, but take care they don't twist together. Work Straight stitches. Try to start and finish all the stitches in the blank area around the printed panel. This will make the edge look neater.

c Stitching in one thread only, work the lace itself as shown in the diagram (see page 48).

d Optional: decorating the lace. Work Couched straight stitches in 2mm quartz ribbon; couch them with French knots. To show the shades of the leaves at the bottom, change to 2mm moss green.

The general look of the lace is shown right. The areas of moss-green stitching can easily be seen. If the ribbon becomes twisted due to multiple French knots worked one by one, there is no need to iron it. Just moisten it a little and it will become flat again. If you moisten it too much, wait until it dries. Working in wet ribbon is not very comfortable and does not seem to give a nice result.

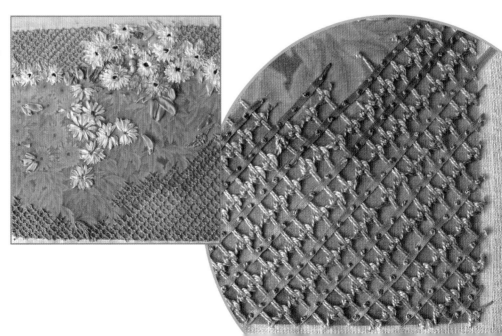

Christmas Rose

The design is based on a watercolour by Catherine Klein (1861–1929).

Finished size: 14 x 21cm (5½ x 8¼in)

Skill level: Beginner

YOU WILL NEED

Stranded cotton thread
• Dark green, white and pale yellow
Needles
• Chenille no. 26 for 2mm ribbon and thread; no. 24 for 2mm ribbon; no. 16 for 7mm and 13mm ribbon; no.13 for 20mm and 25mm ribbon and to make holes in the fabric

Piece of fabric with printed panel for embroidery, see page 199 or find the kit for this design listed as K-064 'Christmas Rose, Helebore' on the author's website (see page 4)

2mm silk ribbon
• 1m (39½in) bright white [1] (hellebore petals)
• 1m (39½in) dark olive (J171) [2] (pine branches)
• 1.5m (59in) olive (S652) [3] (stems and hellebore leaf veins)
• 1.5m (59in) chocolate brown (S675) [4] (wild rose twigs)
• 3.5m (4yd) moss green (S658) [5] (pine branches)
• 5m (5½yd) dark green (J021) [6] (pine branches)

7mm silk ribbon
• 1.2m (47½in) cherry red (S527) [7] (rosehips)
• 1.5m (59in) olive (two shades, S652 and S652D) [8a]+[8b] (stems and hellebore leaves)

13mm silk ribbon
• 60cm (23⅝in) variegated yellow (V039) [9] (hellebores stamens)
• 1.2m (47¼in) bright white [10] (hellebore petals)

20mm silk ribbon
• 80cm (31½in) bright white [11] (hellebore petals)

25mm silk ribbon
• 20cm (8in) bright white [12] (hellebore petals)

Stitches used:

Straight stitch

Padded straight stitch

Whipped straight stitch

Twisted straight stitch; Rope technique

Ribbon stitch (pointed and mallet-shaped)

Side ribbon stitch

Half-bow stitch

Fly stitch

Whipped backstitch

Wasp waist technique

Belt technique

Eyelash technique

Order of work

Read the Getting started chapter on page 8 before beginning. Make a printed panel for this design (see the Designs to transfer section, page 196). The watercolour shows a nice bouquet of pine branches, rosehips and hellebores – commonly known as Christmas rose or winter rose because they blossom in December.

Pine branches

1 2mm dark green [6] and moss green ribbon [5], some dark olive [2]. Dark green stranded cotton thread. Straight stitch, Twisted straight stitch, Rope technique. Embroider pine branches with dark green ribbon and Twisted straight stitches. Then change to moss green and work some more stitches to add a 3D effect. While stitching, try to avoid making the holes in the fabric too big. To achieve this, do not pull on the ribbon too tightly when you complete a stitch. Start stitching each branch from its base and gradually move to the tips. Make sure you don't make long stitches along the back of your embroidery. Start from the upper branches and then move to the bottom of the picture.

Add a more natural look to your artwork: use a dark olive ribbon instead of moss green here and there. And work pine needles on the tips of a few branches using the Rope technique for a 3D effect.

To finish, work some pine needles with stranded cotton thread and Straight stitches.

Hellebore stems and two small leaves

2 2mm and 7mm olive ribbon [3], [8]. Whipped backstitch, Ribbon stitch. Work the stems with Whipped backstitch, changing the ribbon size: use 7mm ribbon for bigger stems and 2mm ribbon for finer ones. A couple of small hellebore leaves are worked with Ribbon stitches and 7mm ribbon.

Rosehips

3 7mm cherry red ribbon [7]. Padded straight stitch. Padded straight stitch means working three Straight stitches on top of each other and doing every stitch a little bit longer than the previous one. The classical shape of the stitch reminds me of the minus sign (-). But this time you will need to shape the padded stitches like the equals sign (=), or even 'more than' or 'less than' signs (< and >) depending on a rosehip shape. Another peculiarity of the padded stitch used for rosehips is that the first of the three stitches is smaller than the other two. The second and the third are the same length, so start and finish them at the same points.

Wild rose twigs

4 2mm chocolate brown ribbon [4]. Twisted straight stitch, Fly stitch, Whipped straight stitch. Start the work at the base of the twigs, moving gradually to their tips. Work several Twisted straight stitches for a twig tip: the stitches should be short enough to do without thread fixation. Work the Fly stitches at the branching points. Where the twigs are thicker, whip the Straight stitches – this helps you to create the right shape for the rose twigs quickly and easily. Using the same ribbon, work several mallet-shaped Ribbon stitches for the tips of the rosehips. Put a sewing pin or fine needle inside the loops of Ribbon stitch to hold them in place, so that they come out very small. Add some Half-bow stitches for a 3D effect.

Hellebore petals

5 2mm, 13mm, 20mm and 25mm bright white ribbon [1], [10], [11], [12]. Straight stitch, Ribbon stitch, Side ribbon stitch, Wasp waist technique, Belt technique. White stranded cotton thread. For petals lying flat on the fabric, use 13mm ribbon to work two Side ribbon stitches facing each other. If necessary, do a tiny Stab stitch on their tips with 2mm ribbon. Use wider ribbon for some of the petals, working them with Straight or Ribbon stitches. Three-dimensional petals are worked with 20mm and 25mm ribbon with either Belt or Wasp waist techniques. You will be more comfortable if you cut a 7cm (2¾in) ribbon length out of 20mm ribbon and a 10cm (4in) length out of 25mm ribbon for the Belt technique. Wasp waist technique, however, is best worked with a normal ribbon length – there is no need to cut it into small pieces.

Hellebore centres

6 13mm variegated yellow ribbon [9]. Eyelash technique. Pale yellow stranded cotton thread. There are three flowers in the design that need embroidered stamens and flower centres. Use different colour shades of variegated silk ribbon to decorate these flowers: I prefer the brightest colours for the central flowers. Cut about 15cm (6in) of ribbon and work the eyelashes as described on page 52. Do not throw away the ribbon threads: instead, use them to fill out the flower centres.

Large hellebore leaves

7 2mm [3] and 7mm olive [8a] + [8b]. Straight stitch, Ribbon stitch, Twisted straight stitch. For these three leaves, use ribbon of a lighter shade of olive for the outer leaves and the darker shade for the leaf in the middle. Work a few Straight and Ribbon stitches for each leaf to create texture. Now change to 2mm ribbon to work long Twisted straight stitches for the leaf veins. Work each leaf vein with several Straight stitches one by one. Thus you will not make them too long and you will avoid needing to fix them with thread.

February Cup

Finished size: 20 x 25cm (8 x 10in)

YOU WILL NEED

Stranded cotton thread
- 60cm (23½in) light yellow
- 30cm (12in) saffron yellow
- 30cm (12in) dark green

DMC pearl cotton size 8 in variegated blues and browns

Needles
- Chenille needles: no.18 for 13mm ribbon, no. 20 for 4mm and 7mm ribbon and no. 24 for 2mm and 4mm ribbon
- No. 10 straw needle for thread embroidery

Piece of fabric with printed panel for embroidery, see page 202 or find the kit listed as K-056 '12 Cups, February' on the author's website (see page 4)

2mm silk ribbon
- 2.5m (2¾yd) spring green (S647) [1] (stems of daffodils, Stem stitch)
- 1m (39½in) hand-dyed bright green [2] (stems of daffodils, whipping of Stem stitch)

4mm silk ribbon
- 30cm (12in) taupe (S665) [3] (spathe)
- 1.2m (47¼in) yellow (S664) [4] (primrose centres)

7mm silk ribbon
- 70cm (27½in) dark green (J021) [5] (primrose leaves)
- 50cm (20in) cherry red (S527) [6] (primrose petals)
- 1.2m (47¼in) saffron yellow (J054) [7] (daffodil corona)
- 1.2m (47¼in) variegated green to olive [8] (leaves)
- 1.5m (59in) sand yellow (S503) [9] (primrose petals and bud)

13mm silk ribbon
- 50cm (20in) dark green (J021) [10] (primrose leaves)
- 50cm (20in) sand yellow (S503) [11] (primrose petals)
- 1.5m (59in) variegated yellow (V039) [12] (daffodil petals)
- 50cm (20in) cherry red (S527) [13] (primrose petals)

Stitches used:

Straight stitch	Zigzag gathering
Arched straight stitch	Wasp waist technique
Looped straight stitch	Ribbon plus technique
Ribbon stitch	Running stitch
Double ribbon stitch	Whipped running stitch
Lazy daisy stitch	Backstitch
French knots	Split stitch
Ruche gathering	Whipped backstitch
Jabot gathering	

The 12 Cups series of designs

Some of my silk ribbon embroidery kits form groups or series because of their common themes. The 12 Cups series is aimed at complete beginners and presents cups filled with seasonal flowers, one for each month. Our favourite flowers are created here in the simplest way possible, teaching the basics of silk ribbon embroidery. It's fun to use a cup instead of a vase or a basket for flowers, isn't it? Besides, it makes a nice kitchen decoration. It also gives you an excellent idea for birthday presents: just think which month you need and stitch the design for that month. It's a kind of floral zodiac! The cups are even painted to remind you of the month in question to complete the picture. Look out for the August and January Cups on pages 164 and 192.

Order of work

Read the Getting started chapter on page 8 before beginning. Make a printed panel for this design (see the Designs to transfer section, page 196).

February brings us a feeling of spring coming soon, which is celebrated in this design. We all love to have spring flowers blossoming on our windowsills, and we often grow daffodils as houseplants and buy tiny pots of primroses to cheer up our winter gloom with their bright colours.

Change the work order shown below if you like. Just be sure you work the underlying parts first.

Daffodil stems and spathes

1 4mm taupe [3], 2mm spring green and bright green ribbon [1], [2]. Ribbon stitch, Double ribbon stitch, Whipped backstitch. Work three spathes in Ribbon and Double ribbon stitch using 4mm taupe ribbon [3]. Now embroider stems in Backstitch, using 2mm spring green silk ribbon [1]. Note that Backstitches should be fairly small, especially where the stem curves. This will help create a smooth stem surface while whipping. Change to bright green [2] and whip the lines of Backstitch.

Daffodil parts

Spathe

Leaf

Stem

Corona

Petal

Daffodil leaves

2 7mm variegated green ribbon [8], green stranded cotton thread. Double ribbon stitch. Select the sections of variegated ribbon you need to work each of the leaves. Trim off the ribbon every time a leaf is finished. That means you cut the ribbon on the back of your work every time a stitch is completed. Leave about 5 to 7mm (¼ to 5⁄16in) of ribbon tail on the back and secure it with thread. Sometimes you also need to fix the tip of a leaf.

Daffodil flowers

Stitching this project does not take much time. However, the few flowers in this design need your very special attention. Do not be in a hurry to shape the petals, as it needs to be done properly.

Petals

3a 13mm variegated yellow ribbon [12], light yellow stranded cotton thread. Ribbon stitch, Wasp waist technique. Make the most of the variegated silk ribbon to show highlights on the flowers: select the right colour shade for each petal. The purple and green lines in the photograph (right) show the structure of daffodil petals. They are gathered in two groups of three, placed in between each other. Try to follow that pattern, stitching the three bottom petals first, and then adding three more in between these. This will make your daffodil look more realistic.

Regarding the stitching technique: each flower has both flat petals (worked in Ribbon stitch) and 3D ones (Wasp waist technique). Work one, two or three dimensional petals for each flower. Their tips are not attached to the fabric, which gives a natural look to the flowers.

Corona

3b 7mm saffron yellow ribbon [7]. Straight stitch. Work two
or three Straight stitches radiating from the base of the corona
as if to form a triangle. To stitch the edge: 7mm saffron yellow
ribbon [7], toning stranded cotton thread. Zigzag gathering.
Work one short row of the gathering across the top of the
corona. Attach it to the fabric using the same thread. The shape
of Zigzag gathering will differ, depending on how tightly you pull
on the thread. Experiment to find your preferred effect.

Daffodil bud

4 7mm green [8], 13mm variegated yellow [12]. Straight stitch,
Ribbon stitch, Ribbon plus technique. Start with the bud petals.
Work them in 13mm ribbon with the Ribbon plus technique.
Firstly make a supporting stitch across the base of the bud.
Now stitch the petals in two or three stitches, bringing your
ribbon under the supporting stitch. This will add relief to the
bud. These stitches could be either Straight or Ribbon stitches.
Change to 7mm green ribbon to work the flower cup and the
spathe in Straight stitches.

Primroses

The four central primroses

5a Petals: 7mm and 13mm cherry red
ribbon [6], [13] and sand yellow ribbon
[9], [11]. Looped straight stitch. To add
interest to your embroidery, work one of
the cherry red primroses in 7mm instead
of 13mm ribbon. To create the width of
the petals, work two stitches for each
petal instead of one. Do the same with
the sand yellow primroses.

Primrose centres: 4mm yellow ribbon [4]. Straight stitch. Work one or two short Straight stitches in 4mm ribbon at the base of each petal. This will add a dash of colour. All the five dashes placed together make up the flower centre. Arrange your own work order: either stitch all the petals first, and then start embroidering in 4mm ribbon, or work a petal, then make a stitch in 4mm ribbon, fixing the petal in its place. Repeat for all the other petals. The latter option is safer, because there is no risk of distorting the petal shape. However, the former one is more comfortable, as you don't need to use two needles at once. A compromise is to use pins to fix all five petals, then remove a pin from the first petal and work a stitch over it. But be careful while pinning the petals: natural silk ribbon is so delicate that even a fine sewing pin might damage its structure. To avoid holes in the ribbon, use pins in parts of the petals which are going to be hidden with 4mm ribbon.

The sideways primrose

5b 7mm sand yellow [9], 7mm dark green ribbon [5]. Straight stitch, Arched straight stitch. For the three petals of this primrose, work six stitches, placing them in groups of two. The last stitch may be worked arched for a 3D effect. Now work the flower cup in Straight stiches using 7mm green ribbon. These stitches should come across the primrose petals a little.

The primrose bud

5c 7mm sand yellow [9] and dark green ribbon [5]. Straight stitch a loop. Work it in a similar way.

Primrose leaves

6 7mm and 13mm dark green ribbon [5], [10]; toning stranded cotton thread. Ruche and Jabot gathering. Work some of the leaves in Jabot gathering technique using 13mm ribbon. The others are Ruche gathering for 7mm ribbon. Do not forget to use one strand of thread only to do this job.

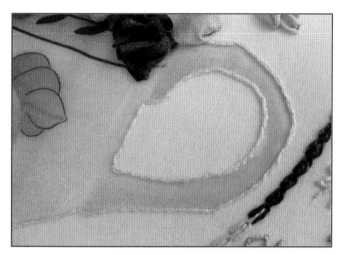

Outlining the cup

7 Light yellow stranded cotton thread. Split stitch. Stitch around the cup contour to add texture. There is no need to outline the cup in bright thread, because it should be in the background of the flower arrangement.

Thread embroidery

8 DMC pearl cotton thread size 8 in variegated blues and browns. The thread embroidery is divided into two parts: one stands for winter and the other for spring. In many countries, February is the time when winter meets spring, and this is the February Cup. Work snowflakes in Straight stitches, weaving around the centre if necessary. For flowers and butterflies, use Lazy daisy stitch and French knots.

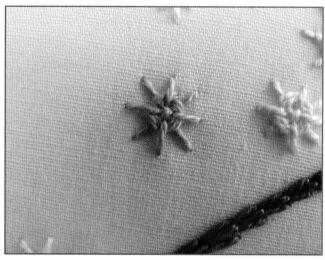

SEASONAL GIFTS

We are all made the same way: we need to have special days in our lives. These might be important moments or treasured events that occur every year – they brighten up our routine existence. How wonderful it is to delight our relatives and friends with gifts from the heart, prepared particularly for a special day.

August Cup, page 164

Mother's Day, page 158

Friendship Heart, page 172

January Cup, page 192

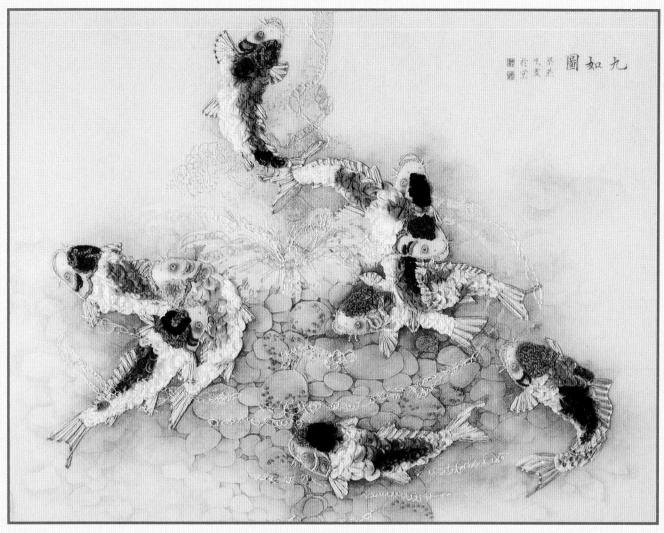

Housewarming Carp, page 182

Christmas Star, page 188

Easter Wreath, page 146

Easter Wreath

The name of the original design is With a Sea-wave. These words are from the Orthodox Easter service read in church on the evening of Easter Saturday before the Resurrection: 'He, who with a sea-wave had buried the tyrant pursuer long ago, was buried beneath the earth by sons of those then delivered…' The green of the flowers is also called 'sea-wave green' in my language, which creates a kind of word play. Of course there are also Easter eggs in the wreath, and it is worked in delicate spring colours.

Skill level: Intermediate

Finished size: 33 x 33cm (13 x 13in)

YOU WILL NEED

Stranded cotton thread
- Sea green, natural white, yellow

Needles
- Chenille needles no.s 16, 18, 20, 26, two no. 24
- Embroidery needle no. 8 or 10

Piece of fabric with transferred template, see pages 148–150, or find the kit for this design listed as K-061 'By Sea Wave (With a Sea-wave)' on the author's website (see page 4)

Linen for the lining

Extra fabric for trapunto embroidery

Sea-green beads or buttons

2mm silk ribbon
- 8m (8¾yd) spring green (S647) [1] (heart-shaped leaves and stems)
- 12m (13¼yd) natural white [2](aeonium)
- 13m (14¼yd) light yellow (S655) [3] (big flower stamens, yellow flowers)
- 17m (18¾) light green (J031) [4] (heart-shaped leaves and aeonium)

4mm silk ribbon
- 1.5m (59in) sand yellow (S503) [5] (Easter eggs)

- 2.3m (2½yd) light green (J031) [6] (narrow flat leaves)
- 2.5m (2¾yd) natural white [7](narrow flat leaves)
- 3m (3½yd) saffron yellow (J054) [8] (Easter eggs)
- 3.5m (4yd) yellow (S664) [9] (Easter eggs)
- 4m (4½yd) light yellow (S655) [10] (Easter eggs)
- 6m (6¾yd) variegated yellow (V039) [11] (big flower stamens and yellow flowers)

7mm silk ribbon
- 30cm (12in) light green (J031) [12] (heart-shaped leaves)
- 2.5m (2¾yd) variegated yellow (V039) [13] (yellow flowers)
- 3.5m (4yd) spring green (S647) [14] (heart-shaped leaves)
- 3.7m (4¼yd) dark green (J021) [15] (big flower sepals)
- 5m (5½yd) hand-dyed green [16] (heart-shaped leaves)

13mm silk ribbon
- 4.5m (5yd) natural white [17] (aeonium)
- 4.5m (5yd) light green (J031) [18] (aeonium)
- 4.6m (5¼yd) variegated sea green (V241) [19] (big flower petals)

Stitches used:

Straight stitch	Trapunto embroidery
Couched straight stitch	Victoria Amazonica technique
Twisted straight stitch, Rope technique	Eyelash technique
Central ribbon stitch	Braid technique
Arched ribbon stitch	Kokeshi doll technique
French knots	Great Wall of China technique
Zigzag gathering	Stem stitch
Wasp waist technique	Whipped backstitch
There-and-back technique	Crochet chain

Order of work

Read the Getting started chapter on page 8 before beginning. The work order is not fixed, but it is recommended to start with the bigger flowers.

The full-size template is shown on the following pages, divided into three parts: the top left on page 148, top right on page 149 and the bottom (rotated to fit) on page 150. Join them together and transfer the template onto the fabric. Compare with the image shown right to identify the elements of the design correctly. While reading the Key (page 151), pay attention to the advice regarding the peculiarities of transferring this design.

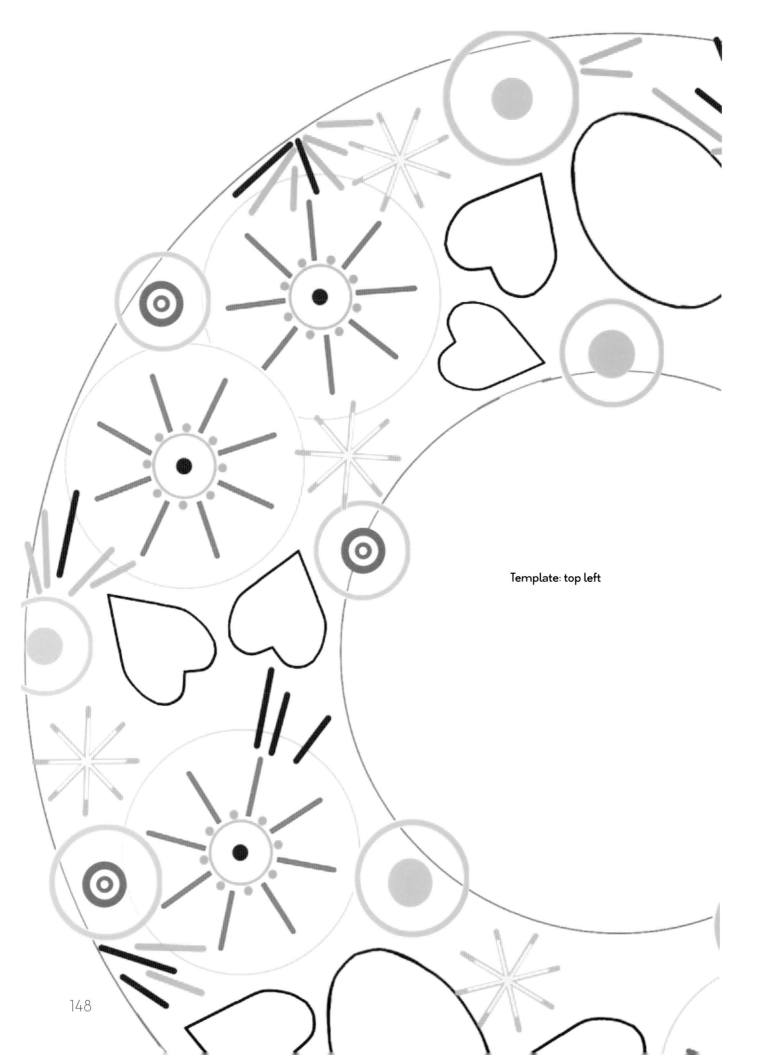

Template: top left

148

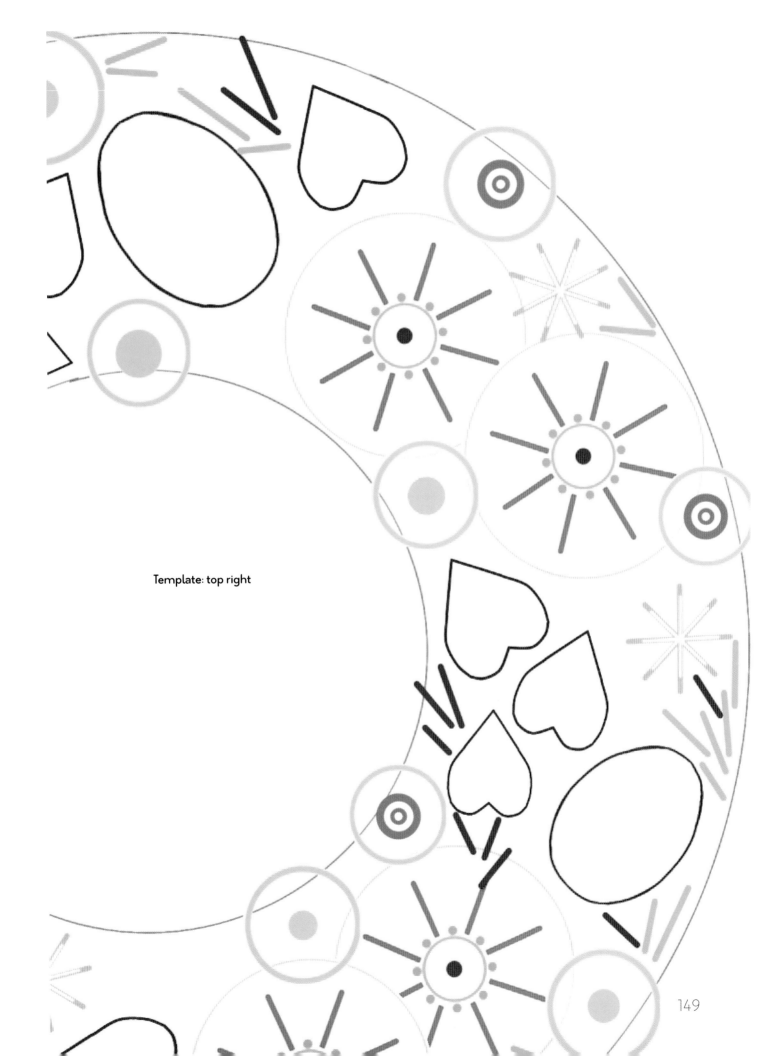

Template: top right

149

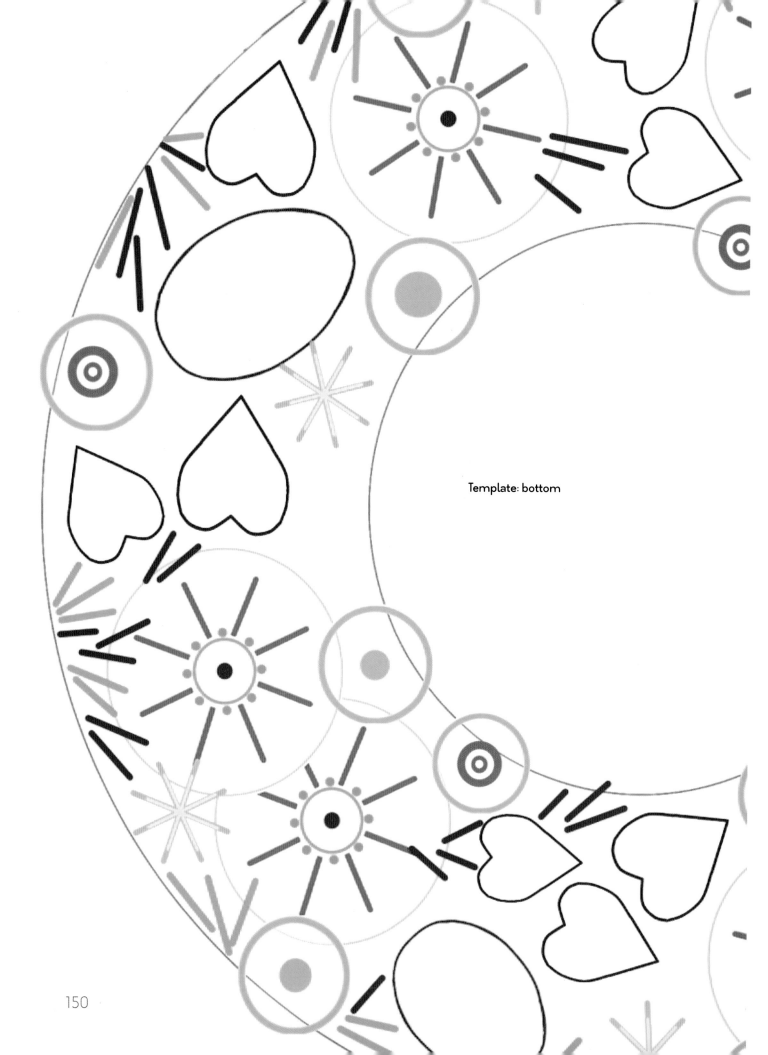

Template: bottom

Key and tips for template

Symbols	Parts of the design	How to transfer them to fabric
	Big sea-green flowers	Do not draw the yellow circle: work a line of Running stitch instead.
	Leaves	Fine line round the heart shape.
	Golden yellow Easter eggs	Fine line around the egg shape.
	Small pale yellow flowers	Eight fine lines radiating from the centre.
	Aeonium in light green ribbon	Draw the outer circle only. Make a mark inside the circle to indicate light green ribbon for stitching.
	Aeonium in white ribbon	Draw the outer circle only. No mark inside the circle for stitching with white ribbon.
	Narrow light green leaves	Fine lines.
	Narrow white leaves	Fine lines.
	Stems	Fine lines. Light green and bright green stems are marked in the same colour. Use the photograph of the finished piece as a guide or work them as you prefer.

 +  +  =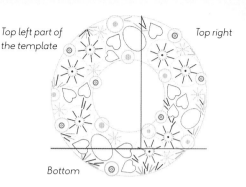

Top left

Top right

Bottom

Top left part of the template

Top right

Bottom

Using the template

These diagrams show the three main parts of the template. Join them together using clear tape and transfer the template onto the fabric. Note that the two top parts of the template go vertically and the bottom part should be turned 90 degrees anticlockwise.

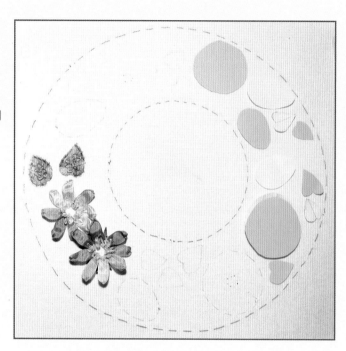

a You will need two pieces of fabric to work this design: the base fabric for stitching and the linen lining to support the stitches. Iron them before you start embroidering.

b Transfer the template onto the base fabric with a soft sharp pencil. This time it is not recommended to use fabric markers, as rinsing the fabric after stitching may distort the 3D petals.

c Do not make pencil marks for the inner and the outer borders of the wreath, as these marks would not be covered with stitches. Work a row of Running stitch around the wreath borders instead. To make the job easier, copy the wreath outlines onto an extra piece of paper or draw a circle on that paper 33cm (13in) in diameter. Cut out the circle, pin it to the base fabric and work a line of Running stitches around it.

d Do a similar job for the sea-green flowers. Cut a paper circle for a flower, referring to the size shown in the template. Pin it to the fabric and work stitching around it in white thread to mark the length of the petals. Mark the bases of the petals with eight dots only. If you have buttons for flower centres, place one of the buttons in the middle of the paper circle and outline it with a pencil. Now place the eight dots on the outline and trace them onto the fabric. Having finished stitching the petals, remove the thread of the Running stitches and continue your embroidery.

e Attach the linen to the base fabric and frame both in your embroidery hoop or frame. This can be done in two different ways: a) Stretch the lining in your hoop/frame drum tight. Now attach the base fabric on top of the lining using Running stitch. This method of stretching works particularly well for delicate base fabrics. Besides, it is a common way to deal with any kind of stretcher bars and similar embroidery frames. b) If your base fabric is not too fine, fix it in your embroidery hoop first and then just attach the lining from the back.

Large sea-green flowers

These flowers are inspired by Collarette dahlias. Use the same stitching technique and work them in their natural colour scheme to create another design, for instance a dahlia bouquet.

Petals

1a 13mm variegated sea-green ribbon [19]. Wasp waist technique. To embroider one flower you will need two lengths of ribbon about 30cm (12in) long. To make your work more comfortable, Stab stitch the bottom of each petal with 2mm light yellow ribbon.

Stamens

1b 2mm light yellow ribbon [3]. Wasp waist technique. Work two or three stamens for each petal. Make the stamens as long as a quarter or a third of the petal length. You will need two lengths of ribbon about 50cm (20in) long. Note that the stamens are supposed to go through the petal bases to fix them. Having finished with 2mm ribbon, move closer to the flower centre to work a circle of stamens with 4mm variegated yellow ribbon [11]. You will need one length about 40cm (16in) long. Work in the same Wasp waist technique but place just one or two stamens per petal. These should also be shorter (see the two red arrows in the photograph, left).

Sepals

1c 7mm dark green ribbon [15]. There-and-back technique. Place the sepals in between the petals (eight red arrows in the photograph). The sepals should reach two-thirds of the petal length.

Centres

1d Use nice-looking buttons or work seed bead embroidery to create the flower centres.

♡ Heart-shaped leaves

The heart-shaped outline

2a 2mm light green ribbon [4] and 7mm hand-dyed green [16]. Victoria Amazonica technique. Starting from the petiole (leaf stalk, wide end), embroider the shape, placing the curl of the Ribbon stitches outside the leaf (see right).

Decoration outside the leaf

2b 2mm light green ribbon [4] and 2mm spring green [1]; 7mm hand-dyed green [16] and 7mm light green [12]. Couched straight stitch, French knots, Eyelash technique. For each leaf choose your own combination of the ribbons and techniques.

Option 1 Couched straight stitches and French knots (to couch them). Use 2mm ribbon only, either shade of green (use the shade shown in the photograph or choose your own). Use two chenille needles and two lengths of ribbon: no. 26 chenille to work the Straight stitches and no. 24 to stitch the French knots.

Option 2 Eyelash technique. Use 7mm ribbon to work the fringe and 2mm ribbon to Stab stitch around a leaf.

Option 3 Use both methods together (see right). Firstly work Couched straight stitches around a leaf and then add a fringe around the whole leaf or just on one side.

The leaf centre

2c 7mm spring green ribbon [14], toning thread. Zigzag gathering. Work a small section of Zigzag stitching, gather the ribbon and place it in the leaf centre. If you are happy with the result, Stab stitch the ribbon in place. If not, work some more Zigzag gathering stitches to enlarge it. The gathering is supposed to be oval-shaped, with its inner scallops overlapping (see left).

◯ Easter eggs

3 4mm ribbon of different shades of yellow [8], [9], [10] and sand yellow [5]. Braid technique; rope worked with Twisted straight stitch; Stem stitch and trapunto embroidery. Create the braids and attach them to the fabric at a different angle for each egg. Change the ribbon colour to show the lit and shaded parts of the egg, thus making it look three-dimensional. Then attach a rope worked with 2mm ribbon around the egg outline. For Trapunto embroidery see the directions on page 49.

Yellow flowers

4 4mm and 7mm variegated yellow ribbon [11], [13]; 2mm light yellow ribbon [3]. Kokeshi doll technique, Centre ribbon stitch, Arched ribbon stitch. Work a pointed Centre ribbon stitch with 7mm ribbon for the lower layer of each petal. Then cover two-thirds of it with a short mallet-shaped Ribbon stitch using 4mm ribbon. Do not forget to place a second needle (no. 24 chenille) inside the stitch roll to prevent it from distorting.

You will be more comfortable using two no. 24 chenilles to support the stitch rolls. Work like this:

- Embroider a ribbon stitch and put one of the chenilles inside its roll.
- Now work a second ribbon stitch, using the second chenille to support the roll.
- For the third stitch take the chenille out of the first Ribbon stitch (there is no need to support it any more) and use it as usual to support the roll.

For the finishing touch, work mallet-shaped Ribbon stitches in 2mm pale yellow on top of the first two petal layers. These stitches are to be the shortest, of course. Work them arched if you like – it will add charm to the flower.

Aeonium

5 Light green and natural white silk ribbon. Each comes in two sizes of 2mm [4], [2] and 13mm [17], [18]. Great Wall of China technique, French knots. Place the wall in a spiral shape. Start working the aeonium from the outer circle, moving steadily to its centre. It seems to be more comfortable for right-handed stitchers to do the job clockwise, while the left-handed should work anticlockwise. This will speed up the work: otherwise it will take about an hour to stitch one aeonium. Regarding the ribbon length: you will need about 70cm (27½in) of 13mm ribbon and 2–2.5m (2¼–2¾yd) of 2mm ribbon to fix the wall and to work the French knots in the centre. Most of the knots are three-loop, but if a gap in between the knots appears, fill it in with smaller (one- or two-wrap) French knots.

Narrow light green and white leaves

6 4mm light green ribbon [6] and 4mm natural white ribbon [7]. There-and-back technique, Ribbon stitch. Vary the ribbon colour as you please or use the photograph of the finished piece as a guide.

Stems

7 2mm spring green ribbon [1]. Whipped backstitch. For convenience sake, it would be wiser to embroider the stems first and then add the flowers and leaves. However the stems are to really here to decorate the whole composition, so it is better to have all the rest stitched when you start working the stems. In this way you will be able to change their position and number to suit your needs.

Outline

8 Sea-green stranded cotton thread or tiny beads – I used sea-green delica MIYUKI DBM626 beads size 10/0 (for the outline); white stranded cotton or silk thread (for the inner contour). French knots; crochet chain stitch. The seed beads used in the original design could be replaced by two- or three-loop French knots worked with two strands of thread. For the inner circle, work crochet chain and attach it with the same thread. Use a size 4 crochet hook (not a fine one) to make the crochet look like sea foam.

Mother's Day

Finished size: 22 x 19.5cm (8⅝ x 7¾in)

Skill level: Beginner

YOU WILL NEED

Stranded cotton thread
- White or pink (to fix petals, the rose and knotted flowers); olive (to attach stems to the fabric)

Golden or pinkish Atlas thread with lustre or any similar kind such as silk, viscose or polyester – it should be like DMC pearl cotton thread size 12, but with lustre (fine twigs)

Pale olive bouclé knitting yarn (stems, twigs)

Needles
- Chenille needle no.13 (to make holes in fabric); no.s 18 and 20 (for ribbon embroidery)
- No.10 embroidery needle (for thread embroidery)

Piece of fabric with printed panel for embroidery, see page 203, or find the kit for this design listed as K-040 'Mother's Day' on the author's website (see page 4)

2mm silk ribbon
- 1m (39½in) olive (S652) [1]
- 1m (39½in) plum (J084) [2]
- 1m (39½in) moss green (S658) [3]
- 3m (3½yd) variegated lilac (V001) [4]

4mm silk ribbon
- 1.5m (59in) saffron yellow (J054) [5]
- 1.5m (59in) light yellow (S655) [6]
- 2m (79in) variegated peach (V101) [7]
- 1.5m (59in) variegated olive (V024) [8]

7mm silk ribbon
- 3m (3½yd) natural white [9]
- 1m (39½in) dusty rose (S565) [10]
- 3m (3½yd) flamingo pink (J022) [11]
- 1m (39½in) pale rose (S558) [12]
- 1.5m (59in) olive (S652) [13]
- 2m (79in) dark olive (J171) [14]
- 1.5m (59in) lavender (J102) [15]
- 1m (39½in) periwinkle (S579) [16]
- 1m (39½in) saffron yellow (J054) [17]

13mm silk ribbon
- 2.5m (2¾yd) natural white [18]

20mm or 25mm silk ribbon
- 1m (39½in) pink (S550) or bright white [19]

Stitches used:

Straight stitch	Feather stitch
Whipped straight stitch	French knot
Twisted straight stitch	Star rose
Eye-looped stitch	Ruche gathering
Big bow stitch	Classical twisted rose
Ribbon stitch	Lazy ruche technique
Reverse ribbon stitch	Knotted flowers
Half-bow stitch	Puffy petals
Lazy daisy stitch	Ribbon plus technique
Twisted daisy stitch	Plumeria technique
Fly stitch	Kokeshi doll technique

Order of work

Read the Getting started chapter on page 8 before beginning. Make a printed panel for this design (see the Designs to transfer section, page 196). Flowers appear in the instructions as marked in this photograph. The order of stitching is not fixed.

The four five-petal flowers

The Puffy petal flowers

1a These are worked in 13mm white ribbon [18] in Puffy petal technique. To dye the flowers, apply some clean water to the petal you are going to dye. Mix watercolour paints to get the necessary shade. Use baby pink for the middle part of the petals of the pink flower and pale blue for the ends of the pink flower. Use a hairdryer to dry the ribbon. Note: the wet spot should ALWAYS be bigger than the space you are going to dye (or you will get an ugly tidemark showing the border between dry and wet ribbon). Work one- or two-loop French knots for the centre, using 7mm saffron yellow ribbon [17].

The pink flower

1b Work the petals in Ribbon plus technique using 7mm white ribbon [9]. Stitch the flower centres in Star rose with 7mm saffron yellow [17]. Note that the [9] ribbon works for both stitching and supporting for the Ribbon plus technique. Dye the petals with watercolour paints, having mixed white and scarlet.

The plumeria flower

1c Use 13mm natural white [18] for the Plumeria technique. Work five Ribbon stitches (mallet-shaped). These five rolls should be twisted at an angle and fixed with white thread and tiny stitches. Apply some water to the ends of the petals and dye them with blue to lilac watercolour. Work a cluster of French knots in 4mm saffron [5] for the flower centre.

Three-part rose

Combine different stitching techniques to get a totally new rose shape!

Rose centre

2a Work Classical twisted rose first, using 20mm or 25mm pink ribbon [19]. Stop adding to it while it looks like a rosebud, as this is only for the central part of the flower, not for the whole rose. Using a no. 13 chenille needle, make a hole in the fabric and bring the bottom part of the Classical twisted ribbon rose to the back. Stab stitch it with thread.

Rose petals

2b These are Whipped straight stitches, placed around the centre of the rose. Use 7mm ribbon of different shades of pink [10, 11, 12].

The surrounding petals

2c These are worked in Lazy ruche technique, using 7mm white ribbon [9]. Place the ruche around the rose and fix with thread. Apply some clean water and dye the rose petals. To prevent the paint from dyeing the fabric, put a paper towel in between the fabric and the ruche. Use a hairdryer to dry it.

Knotted flowers

3 7mm flamingo pink ribbon [11] and Knotted flower technique.

Puffy flowers

4 Here is one more idea to speed up your embroidery process. Wind a full length of ribbon around your forefinger, take it off carefully and fix it, stitching through all the loops, just at one point. Attach it to the fabric. Use 2mm variegated lilac ribbon [4].

Knotted roses

5 Using 7mm lavender silk ribbon [15], work Star roses. To make the loops tighter while keeping the central part three-dimensional, stitch the finished rose top to bottom using 2mm variegated lilac ribbon [4]. One Stab stitch through the rose centre will do nicely: just go up and down. Follow the photograph. These roses are surrounded by tiny flowers worked in Lazy daisy stitches, using 2mm variegated lilac ribbon [4]. Five stitches radiating from the centre form pretty flowers to complement the roses: these flowers are flat, but the roses are three-dimensional. Both are worked in the same colour, adding depth to the bouquet.

Buttercups

6 Work these in 4mm saffron [5] and light yellow [6] ribbon. Embroider five Central ribbon stitches radiating from the flower centre. These tiny delicate flowers are the perfect background for the other three-dimensional parts of the bouquet. There is no need to work French knots in the centres of these buttercups.

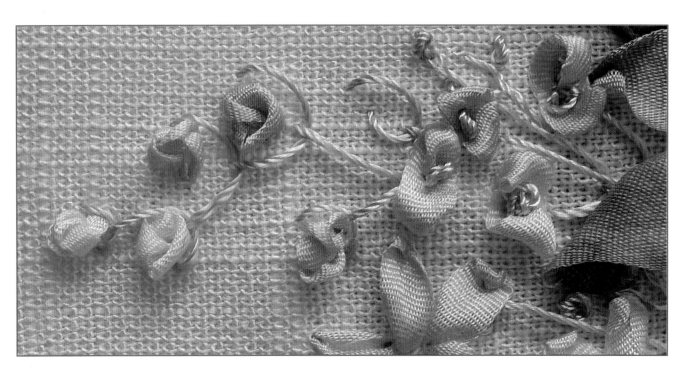

Variegated twigs

7 These are shown by the light green dotted line in the Order of work image on page 159. They are worked using 4mm variegated peach ribbon [7], in French knots and Half-bow stitches. Flowers at the bottom are bigger. The twigs themselves are worked in Fly stitch and Feather stitch in golden thread with lustre.

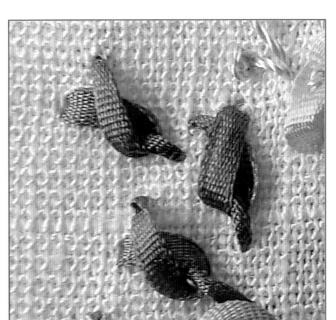

Small buds

8 2mm plum ribbon [2]. Twisted daisy stitch can be placed in the opposite direction (the fixing stitch at the bottom). This was a new discovery for me!

Leaves and flower stems

9 Work Ribbon stitch in 2mm, 4mm and 7mm ribbon of different shades of green [1, 3, 8, 13, 14]. Work Twisted straight stitches for the stems, using the same ribbon or attach olive bouclé knitting yarn to the fabric for some of the stems. Fix them in places with olive stranded cotton thread, working short Stab stitches. Sometimes it is possible to use narrow silk ribbon to fix them (see the red arrow in the photograph). Work some leaves, placing Ribbon stitches on top of each other (Kokeshi doll technique, see page 53).

The bow

10 7mm periwinkle ribbon [16], Big bow stitch. Just one peculiarity: work one more Straight stitch on top of one of the bow loops. Look at the free ribbon ends in the photograph – they are stitched in a different way. One of them is attached to the fabric (Ribbon stitch), and the other is three-dimensional, with its end cut at an angle. Use fine-pointed sharp scissors to cut it this way.

August Cup

This design was specially developed to celebrate people born in summer, when many loved ones are away on vacation and can't make it to a birthday party. The flowers are displayed in a cup instead of a vase: learn more about 12 Cups series of embroidery designs on page 139.

Finished size: 28 x 21cm (11 x 8¼in)

Skill level: Beginner

YOU WILL NEED

Stranded cotton thread
- Two shades of green and greyish blue DMC pearl cotton thread size 8)

Woollen thread or a rope made from several strands of stranded cotton thread (see the rope method, page 22)

Needles
- Chenille needles: no.s 16 and no. 18 for 7mm and 13mm; no.s 20, 24 and 26 for 2mm and 4mm ribbon
- No. 10 embroidery needle (for thread embroidery)

Piece of fabric with printed panel for embroidery, see page 204, or find the kit for this design listed as K-042 '12 Cups, August' on the author's website (see page 4)

2mm silk ribbon
- 50cm (20in) deep periwinkle blue (S581) [1] (delphinium)
- 1m (39½in) black [2] (sunflower centres)
- 60cm (23½in) olive green (S652) [3] (sunflower leaves)
- 60m (23½in) dark olive (J171) [4] (sunflower leaves)
- 60cm (23½in) moss green (S658) [5] (sunflower leaves)
- 70cm (27½in) variegated olive (V024) [6] (leaves along the stems of pink flowers)
- 1m (39½in) variegated blue to yellow (V247) [7] (delphinium)
- 1.2m (47½in) peach (S514) [8] (little flowers)
- 1.8m (71in) light yellow (S655) [9] (flowers of Rhodiola rosea)

4mm silk ribbon
- 50cm (20in) moss green (S658) [10] (leaves of rhodiola rosea)
- 50cm (20in) olive (S652) [11] (leaves of rhodiola rosea)
- 60cm (23½in) dark blue (S584) [12] (delphinium flowers)
- 1.5m (59in) variegated blue to yellow (V247) [13] (delphinium)
- 60cm (23½in) brown (S668) [14] (flowers of rhodiola rosea)
- 1.2m (47½in) saffron yellow (J054) [15] (flowers of rhodiola rosea)
- 1.2m (47½in) variegated light emerald green (V241) [16] (twigs)
- 1.2m (47½in) scarlet (S554) [17] (small flowers)
- 2m (79in) variegated scarlet (V028) [18] (pink flowers with Star rose centres)

7mm silk ribbon
- 20cm (8in) variegated light emerald green (V241) [19] (twigs)
- 50cm (20in) dark blue (S584) [19a] (delphinium flowers)
- 60cm (23½in) variegated blue to yellow (V247) [19b] (delphinium flowers)
- 1m (39½in) olive green (S652) [20] (sunflower leaves)
- 1m (39½in) dark olive (J171) [21] (sunflower leaves)
- 1m (39½in) moss green (S658) [22] (sunflower leaves)
- 1m (39½in) dark green (J021) [23] (delphinium leaves)
- 3m (3½yd) black [24] (sunflower centres: the ribbon should be divided into three equal parts for three flowers)

13mm silk ribbon
- 30cm (12in) dark blue (S584) [25] (delphinium flowers)
- 50cm (20in) deep periwinkle blue (S581) [26] (delphinium flowers)
- 1m (39½in) variegated blue to yellow (V247) [27] (delphiniums)
- 1.2m (47½in) pale pink (S558) [28] (pink flowers with Star rose centres: the ribbon should be divided into three equal parts for three flowers)
- 2m (79in) light yellow (S655) [29] (sunflower petals)
- 70cm (27½in) yellow (S664) [29a] (sunflower petals)
- 50cm (20in) peach (S514) [29b] (sunflower petals)
- 1.8m (71in) yellowish to brown, hand-dyed [30] (sunflower petals)

Stitches used:

Straight stitch
Padded straight stitch
Arched straight stitch
Looped straight stitch
Twisted straight stitch
Ribbon stitch
Looped ribbon stitch

Double ribbon stitch
Half-bow stitch
Lazy daisy stitch
Fly stitch
Spider web rose
French knot
Pistil stitch

Backstitch
Split stitch
Victoria Amazonica technique
Star rose
Whipped backstitch

Order of work

Read the Getting started chapter on page 8 before beginning. Make a printed panel for this design (see the Designs to transfer section, page 196). Start with the bigger flowers.

Three sunflowers

Centres

1a 2mm and 7mm black ribbon [2] and [24]. Spider-web rose. Use 2mm ribbon to work the web. It should result in five lines (stitches) coming out from the centre. Now take 7mm ribbon and do the weaving: starting from the centre, go over one stitch and under the next one, etc. Follow this rule until the rose is complete. When I worked these three sunflower centres, I found that a slight twisting of the 7mm ribbon before stitching works even better for this design. (See Twisted straight stitch, page 22).

Petals

1b 13mm yellow [29a] as well as hand-dyed yellow silk ribbon [30] (and some 13mm light yellow [29] and 13mm peach [29b] if you want to add a different shade. Straight stitch, Ribbon stitch. The stitches should radiate from the centre. The first stitch is a Ribbon stitch, and it starts near the flower centre coming to the outer edge. Then work a Straight stitch from the outer edge to the centre to save the ribbon and to prevent too long stitches forming on the back of the fabric. The back is shown in the photograph (left). Or you can work all petals in Ribbon stitch. If so, cut the ribbon tail after each petal is finished.

Green leaves

1c 2mm and 7mm ribbon of different shades of green [3], [4], [5], [20], [21] and [22]. Ribbon stitch, Victoria Amazonica technique.

Victoria leaves in this design have some peculiarities:
• **Ribbon colour** Each leaf is worked in 7mm ribbon of three different shades of green. The top part of the leaves is embroidered in the darkest green. The middle is formed by olive green ribbon, and the tip is light olive ribbon. Change the colour of 2mm supporting ribbon every time you change the colour of the stitching ribbon.

- **Shaping the leaf tips** See steps 1 to 3 showing how to stitch the leaf tip. Note that this time the 2mm ribbon goes through the 7mm ribbon. The red dot in step 3 shows where the 7mm ribbon goes through itself, forming a Ribbon stitch curl.

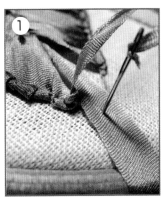  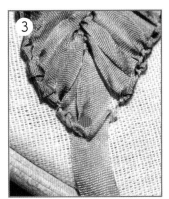 

Delphinium

Flowers

2a 2mm, 4mm, 7mm and 13mm ribbon of blue to yellow variegated [7], [13], [19b], [27]; 2mm and 13mm deep periwinkle blue [1], [26]; 4mm, 7mm and 13mm dark blue ribbon [12], [19a], [25]. Half-bow stitch and French knots. Use the photographs as a guide for stitches and ribbon colours. The narrower ribbon is for flowers on the top and the wider ribbon for the lower ones.

Twigs

2b Stranded cotton thread of two shades of green. Fly stitch. Use a darker thread shade for stitches at the bottom.

Green leaves

2c 7mm dark green [23]. Double ribbon stitch. Vary its length to shape the leaf and make the stitches radiate from the centre.

Rhodiola rosea

Flowers

3a 4mm ribbon: brown [14], saffron yellow [15]; 2mm light yellow [9]. Half-bow stitch, French knot, Pistil stitch. Use the photographs as a guide to ribbon colours.

Stems and leaves

3b 4mm ribbon: moss green [10] and olive [11]. Backstitch and Lazy daisy stitch. Work each stem in stranded cotton, using two strands at a time. Now add some Lazy daisy stitch leaves at the bottom of the stem. Use two shades of green to show the depth and make your embroidery three-dimensional.

Pink flowers

Stems

4a Woollen thread or stranded cotton. Straight stitch. Work each stem in the thickest thread. If using stranded cotton, use six threads for one stem. There is no need to fix the stems with a toning thread. The 2mm ribbon used for leaves will do it for you: just start some of the leaves by stitching through the woollen thread.

Leaves

4b 2mm variegated olive ribbon [6]. Ribbon stitch. Embroider the left-hand leaves first, going up the stem. Continue working, going down the stem and embroidering the right-hand leaves. This will make the stitches which are formed on the back of the fabric shorter.

Flowers

4c 4mm variegated pink to scarlet ribbon [18] and 13mm pale pink ribbon [28]. Ribbon stitch and Star rose. Start with 4mm ribbon. Work Ribbon stitches radiating around the centre, leaving some free space inside. Let the stitches lie flat on the fabric. Now change to 13mm ribbon, working a Star rose inside each flower. This will make the flowers dimensional and fill the empty flower centre.

Twigs with emerald-green leaves

5 4mm and 7mm variegated light emerald green [16], [19]. Ribbon stitch. Follow the same rule as shown before to embroider Ribbon stitch leaves on one side of a stem, then on the other side to save ribbon and avoid forming too long stitches on the back of the fabric. Note that the stem is not embroidered here at all to make the twigs a modest background, emphasising the central elements of the composition.

Five-petal scarlet flowers

6 4mm scarlet ribbon [17]. Ribbon stitch, radiating from the centre. Try to make all five stitches the same length. It is also possible to work one Ribbon stitch on top of the other to make the petal puffy.

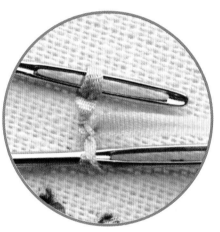

Small lacy peach flowers

7 2mm peach ribbon [8]. Looped straight stitch and Looped ribbon stitch. Take several needles of any kind (not necessarily all chenille needles) or several toothpicks to help you shape the stitches. Leave them in the loops to avoid damaging them while you do the next stitches. I found that in this situation it is worth leaving in two or even three toothpicks so that you don't lose the loops.

The cup

8 Use greyish-blue stranded cotton thread or DMC pearl cotton. Whipped backstitch or Split stitch. Trapunto embroidery technique.

The author at the Bead & Button show in Milwaukee WI with a display including the August Cup project.

Friendship Heart

Stitches used:

Straight stitch
Couched straight stitch
Ribbon stitch
Star rose
Fly stitch
French knot
Colonial knot
Chain stitch
Button rose (Flat rose)
technique
Woven circle filling needlelace
Braid technique

This design was originally part of a series called Heart Windows. They say each person's heart is like a house with a window in it. The house holds that person's moods and emotions. Looking through the window, we can see what treasures are hidden inside. This is how we get to know what the other person's heart is going through. The design show all this in the language of flowers. What do people see in your heart? And which heart do you feel like creating for your mother or child?

The Heart Windows are all small designs, each filled out with one kind of flowers. The technique is aimed at beginners, but each heart has its own special embroidery style.

Finished size: 11 x 10cm (4¼ x 4in)

Skill level: Beginner

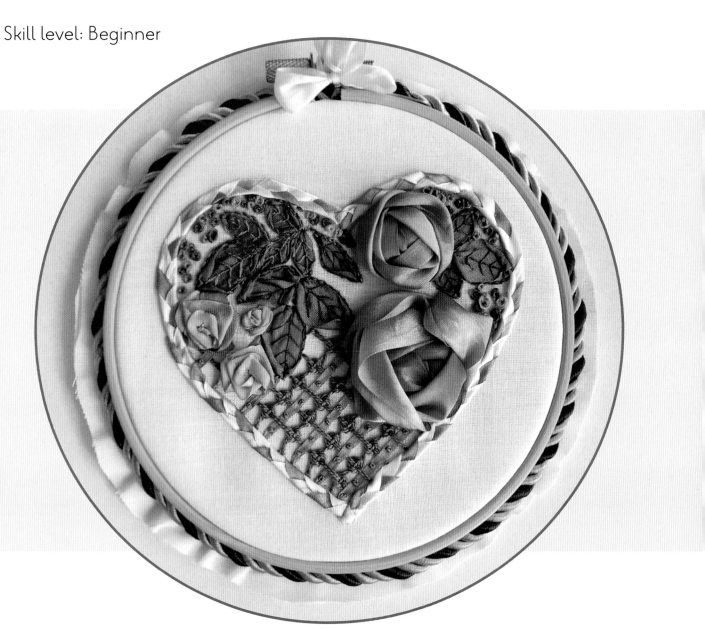

YOU WILL NEED

Stranded cotton thread
- Olive (leaf veins and French knots for background); dark green (leaf veins and French knots for background); pale red, pink or orange/yellow (to fix the roses)

DMC pearl cotton thread size 8
- Greyish green (for needlelace)

Needles
- Chenille needles: no.18 for 7mm and 13mm ribbon; no. 24 for 2mm and 4mm ribbon
- No.10 straw needle for thread embroidery

Piece of light cotton fabric with transferred template, see right, or find the kit for this design listed as K-053 'Heart Windows, Roses' on the author's website (see page 4)

2mm silk ribbon
- 1m (39½in) quartz (S665) [1] (embroidery on top of needlelace,Straight stitches and French knots)

4mm silk ribbon
- 1m (39½in) natural white [2] (braids around the heart)
- 1m (39½in) pale yellow (S655) [3] (braids around the heart)
- 1m (39½in) variegated scarlet (V028) [4] (braids around the heart)

7mm silk ribbon
- 30cm (12in) olive (S652) [5] (leaves)
- 30cm (12in) dark green (J021) [6] (leaves)
- 1m (39½in) hand dyed orange-yellow-pink [7] (three small roses)

13mm silk ribbon
- 30cm (12in) olive (S652) [8] (leaves)
- 30cm (12in) dark green (J021) [9] (leaves)

20mm silk ribbon
- 1m (39½in) hand dyed orange-yellow-pink [10] (two big roses)

Order of work

Read the Getting started chapter on page 8 before beginning. Transfer the template below onto the fabric.

Preparation

1 Iron the fabric and transfer the heart onto it, tracing around it with a soft HB pencil. It is not recommended to use water soluble marker for this purpose because you are going to stitch with hand-dyed ribbon and it might bleed while you are dissolving the lines. If you would like to use it, dissolve the lines before you start stitching. Work a line of Running stitch around the heart and then moisten the fabric with cold water to dissolve the marker lines.

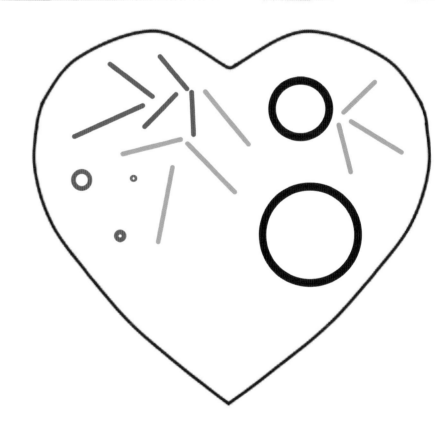

Now you have a heart shape marked onto your fabric. The next step is to make marks for roses and leaves. You can follow the template but the design itself is very simple and the area is small – so it should be really easy to create your own pattern. While tracing it, try to avoid making too many marks – just draw a couple of lines for leaf veins and some dots for rose centres.

Rose leaves

2 7mm and 13mm olive [5, 8] and dark green [6, 9] ribbon. Toning stranded cotton thread. Ribbon stitch, Straight stitch, Fly stitch, Chain stitch. Follow the photographs for a step-by-step guide to working the leaves. Think of the placement of the three rose leaves: either copy this design or work out your own. Mark a line on the fabric for each leaf. Work a Centre ribbon stitch along each line. The leaves are of two shades of green. Thread the needle with a toning thread and work Fly stitches along the leaf veins. The photographs show a way to make the job easier: work a Straight stitch along the central vein of the leaf and then add Fly stitches for smaller veins. Step 6 is optional: add some scallops in chain stitch around some of the leaves for a detailed finish. Change the thread colour to match the ribbon.

The two big roses

3 20mm hand-dyed ribbon [10]. Toning thread. Button rose (Flat rose) technique. Work one of the roses smaller and the other one bigger.

The three small roses

4 7mm hand-dyed ribbon [7]. Star rose stitch. Vary the number of the petals for these roses to make them all different sizes.

The background: knots

5 Olive and dark olive stranded cotton thread. Two- or three-wrap French knots (see below). Work them in two threads and do not pull tightly on the thread. Scatter the knots at random. Vary the threads or combine different colours.

The background: needlelace

6 2mm quartz ribbon [1]. Greyish green DMC pearl cotton thread or similar. Woven circle filling needlelace, Couched straight stitch, French knots. Work the needlelace to cover the area with an intricate texture and to add a flat element to your design. The space between the stitches of the needlelace is about 1 x 1cm (⅜ x ⅜in).

TIP

To add interest, the Couched straight stitches worked in 2mm quartz silk ribbon were worked in between the stitches of the needlelace. The Straight stitches are couched with French knots.

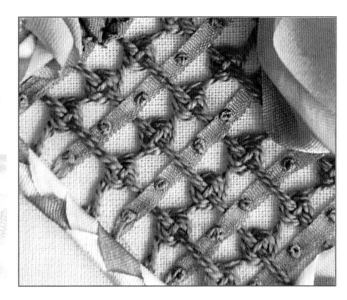

Braid edging

7 4mm natural white [2], pale yellow [3] and variegated scarlet [4]. Braid technique. Attach the braids as shown in the diagram (left). Bring the three lengths of ribbon to the right side of the fabric at the top of the heart (the green dot). Work the braid, going round the left-hand half of the heart (the green arrow). Bring all the ribbon tails down to the back of the fabric at the pointed tip of the heart. Now bring all the three ribbon tails to the right side again close to where they came down. Plait the braid for the right half of the heart (the orange arrow) and go down at the top (near the place marked with the green dot). Working in this way will enable you to create a neat heart shape. This is a very simple yet effective method. Use it for other embroidery designs – for instance work the braids with ribbon of different shades of brown and attach them to the fabric row by row for a basket shape. Three ribbon colours are given above for braids. If you have leftover ribbon, play around with colours to create a heart of your own.

Wedding Day

Finished size: 27 x 26cm (10½ x 10¼in)

Skill level: Intermediate

'They have always been together. Then they met in a museum.' A six-year-old boy's account of how his parents got to know each other.

In my country, autumn was historically considered the right time for a wedding, with harvesting over and less work to do around the farm.

This design can be used for different purposes. It makes a lovely decoration for the cover of a wedding album. You can also add monograms of the newly-weds inside the heart shape and make a wall-hanging for a memorable gift. Finally, if you reduce the size to 15 x 15cm (6 x 6in), this design will make a lovely stitched wedding ring cushion!

YOU WILL NEED

Stranded cotton thread
- White (to anchor the ribbon tails and trace the heart shape)

Needles
- Chenille needles: no. 16 for 13mm ribbon; no. 18 for 7mm ribbon, no. 24 for 2mm and 4mm ribbon, no. 26 for 2mm ribbon and thread

Natural silk and silk organza fabric for stitching through both layers, with transferred template on the silk, or find the kit for this design listed as K-054 'Wedding Time' on the author's website (see page 4)

Fine cotton fabric for the backing

2mm silk ribbon
- 13m (14¼yd) bright white

4mm silk ribbon
- 15m (16½yd) bright white

7mm silk ribbon
- 9m (10yd) bright white

13mm silk ribbon
- 9m (29ft 6in) bright white

13mm silk ribbon
- 50cm (20in) bright white

20mm silk ribbon
- 50cm (20in) bright white

25mm silk ribbon
- 1.5m (59in) bright white

32mm silk ribbon
- 50cm (20in) bright white

Stitches used:

Straight stitch	French knots	Whipped running stitch
Arched straight stitch	Pistil stitch	Victoria Amazonica technique
Looped straight stitch	Ruche gathering	Eyelash technique
Twisted straight stitch	Cherry blossom gathering	Wasp waist technique
Padded straight stitch	Lazy daisy stitch	Goose foot technique
Ribbon stitch	Running stitch	Triangles in a square technique

Order of work

Read the Getting started chapter on page 8 before beginning. Enlarge the template to the correct size. Transfer it carefully onto the silk fabric. Check that the heart shape is nicely rounded. Cut it out from the paper along the lines of the inner and outer heart shapes. Now pin it to the fabric again and work two lines of Running stitch with any light-coloured thread around the paper shape. While stitching the outline with silk ribbon, remove the thread section by section. The work order suggested below is not fixed – you can vary it. The numbers in the diagram are featured as they appear in the Order of work (e.g. number 3 in the diagram indicates primroses).

Peonies

In spite of the step-by-step guide given overleaf, creativity is definitely to be encouraged when you are creating a peony!

Large peony

4mm, 13mm and 25mm ribbon. Straight stitch, Looped straight stitch, Ribbon stitch, Ruche gathering.

1a Work three to four Straight stitches in 13mm ribbon (yellow arrows in the diagram).

1b Work five to six Looped straight stitches in 4mm ribbon (some loops in 2mm ribbon may be added as well). Attach them along the flower centre. You can even divide them into two groups and fix them right and left of centre (purple and blue lines). Make sure the loops are the same size as the Straight stitches. Attach them to the fabric at the bottom of these stitches – the loops will appear a bit shorter than the Straight stitches.

1c Work two or three Straight and/or Ribbon stitches in 13mm ribbon going crosswise. Place them to hide the base of the loops (scarlet and crimson arrows).

1d Work two to five Straight stitches in 25mm ribbon. Let the ribbon go straight or work a little gathering (without pulling on the thread tightly) along one of its selvages (green lines).

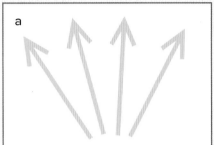

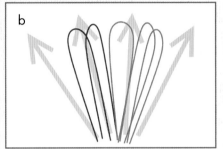

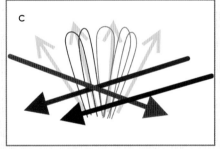

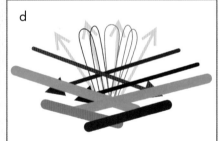

Medium peony

1e 13mm and 25mm ribbon. Straight stitch, Arched straight stitch, Twisted straight stitch. Work the flower following Steps A, B and D of for the Large peony. Twist some of the Straight stitches if you like. Be creative and follow the shape of a real peony.

Peony buds

Large buds

2a 32mm ribbon. White stranded cotton thread. Straight stitches, Triangles in a square technique. See page 40 to work the buds using the Triangles in a square technique. Attach each bud sideways to the fabric and add some petals from the protruding side of the bud in Straight stitches.

Small buds

2b 25mm ribbon. White stranded cotton thread. Straight stitches, Triangles in a square technique. Work in a similar way to the large buds.

Primroses

3a 4mm and 13mm ribbon. Straight stitch, Wasp waist technique. Work two Straight stitches for each petal of a primrose using 13mm ribbon. Work a shorter Straight stitch in 4mm ribbon at the base of each petal. These stitches are both to fix the 13mm Ribbon stitches and to create the primrose flower centre. Use Wasp waist technique for some of the petals to make them three-dimensional.

Sideways primroses

3b 4mm and 13mm ribbon. Straight stitch, Wasp waist technique. Work in a similar way to that described in 3a, just make three petals instead of five.

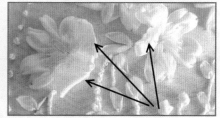

Pear blossom

4 2mm and 7mm ribbon. Looped straight stitch, Victoria Amazonica technique. Those petals lying flat on the fabric are worked with 2mm ribbon in Victoria Amazonica technique. The three-dimensional petals are Looped straight stitches with 7mm ribbon. Stab stitch in white cotton thread at the base of the 7mm loops to fix their shape.

Cherry blossom

5 7mm ribbon, white stranded cotton thread. Cherry blossom gathering, Eyelash technique. Leave five spaces in between the peaks of the gathering to form five petals for each flower. The width of each space varies from 15mm (⅝in) to 20mm (¾in). The wider the space, the fluffier the petals will appear. Work all five spaces the same size. Having worked the Running stitch for the gathering, pull on the thread tightly to form a flower. Attach flowers to the fabric where there are yellow dots in the template. For stamens, cut a 3–4cm (1¼–1½in) length of 13mm ribbon and work Eyelashes. Fold in half several times to create a sort of tassel. Attach the tassel in the flower centre. Trim the ends if necessary.

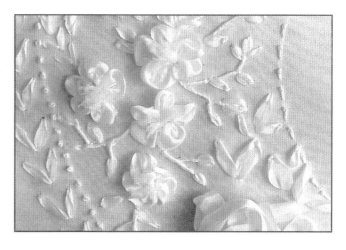

Twigs, normal stitching

6 2mm and 4mm ribbon. Whipped running stitch. Use 4mm ribbon for bigger twigs and 2mm for finer ones. Work Running stitch with longer stitches on the right side of the fabric and short stitches – about 1mm (1/32in) on the back. This will make whipping easier.

Decorative twigs

7 2mm and/or 4mm ribbon. French knots. Work a knotted line imitating a textured twig. Use 4mm ribbon for thicker twigs and 2mm for finer twigs.

Leaves

8 2mm, 4mm and 7mm ribbon. Ribbon stitch and Lazy daisy stitch. Use 7mm ribbon for rose leaves and 4mm ribbon for bigger leaves on the twigs, working both in Ribbon stitch. The smallest leaves are Lazy daisy stitches in 2mm ribbon.

Twigs with buds

9 4mm ribbon. Padded straight stitch. Work several Straight stitches on top of each other. Optional: you can also stitch a French knot covered by several Straight stitches for a more distinct shape.

Leaf border

Wide leaf border

10a This is shown below. 2mm and 7mm ribbon. Ribbon stitch, Goose foot technique. Work a Ribbon stitch for each leaf in 7mm ribbon. The placement of the leaves is shown in the template (page 177) in bold olive lines. Anchor the base of each stitch with three shorter Ribbon stitches worked in 2mm ribbon. These stitches fan along the leaf.

Narrow leaf border

10b Shown on the right. 2mm ribbon. Ribbon stitch. Work pairs of Ribbon stitches without any anchoring.

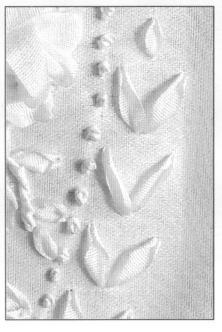

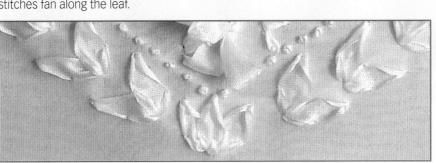

The heart outline

The outer outline

11a The external heart shape. 4mm ribbon. One-wrap French knots. Work the stitches, spacing them evenly along the heart outline. Remove the Running stitches worked in thread as you go. Try to make the right and left-hand parts of the heart symmetrical.

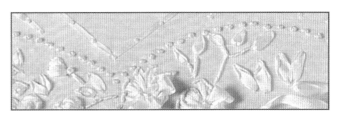

The inner outline

11b 2mm ribbon. One-wrap Pistil stitch. Place the stitches in a similar way to the French knots. Again, try to work the two halves symmetrically.

181

House-warming Carp

This design is based on a traditional Chinese watercolour (guohua) painting by Liang Yan Sheng. Koi carp were originally farmed to put food on the table for poor peasants in the highlands of Japan. At that time most koi carp were a plain pale grey, but some mutant fish had colourful spots on their backs. The Japanese started to breed the latter, keeping them more like pets, while fish without spots were still grown for food. Beauty saves lives!

   The word 'koi' in Japanese also means 'love'. If you find it hard to think of appropriate house-warming gifts for friends who have moved home, why not work this whole design as a wall-hanging for them? Then you can stitch just one fish to make a gorgeous brooch or pendant, to give away or keep for yourself!

Finished size: 36 x 26cm (14¼ x 10¼in)

Skill level: Advanced

Stitches used:

Straight stitch	Whipped backstitch
Twisted straight stitch	Backstitch
Ribbon stitch	Split stitch
Raised ribbon stitch	Victoria Amazonica
Rudbeckia ribbon stitch	technique
Lazy daisy stitch	Crochet chain
Zigzag gathering	Lazy ruche technique
Running stitch	Trapunto embroidery

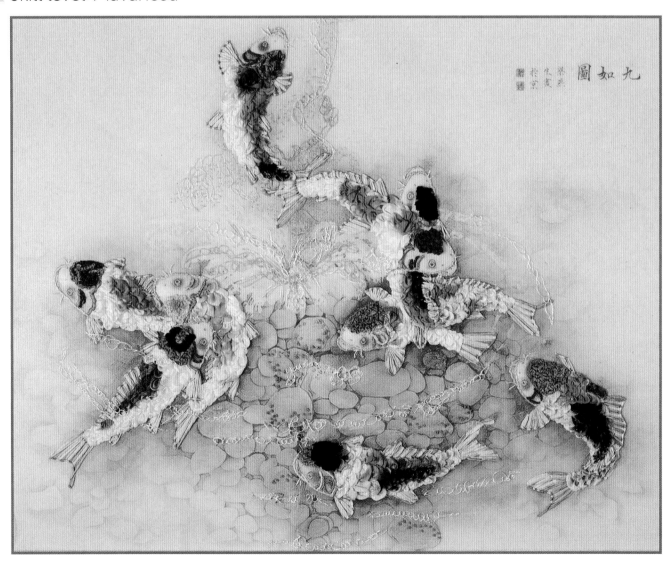

YOU WILL NEED

Stranded cotton thread
- 4m (13ft 1½in) white; some grey, black, crimson, peach

White silk thread for embroidery

Grey DMC pearl cotton thread size 8

Needles
- Chenille needles: three no. 26 for 2mm ribbon, one no. 18 for 7mm, 10mm and 13mm ribbon
- No. 10 embroidery

Piece of fabric with printed panel for embroidery, see page 205, or find the kit for this design listed as K-047 'Koi Carp' on the author's website (see page 4)

2mm silk ribbon
- 2m (79in) peach (S514) [1] (carp heads)
- 3m (3½yd) crimson (S554) [2] (carp heads)
- 3m (3½yd) black [3] (carp heads)
- 9m (10yd) light yellow (S664) [4] (carp fins)
- 15m (16½yd) taupe (S665) [5] (carp fins)
- 9m (10yd) variegated olive (V024) [6] (carp fins)
- 3m (3½yd) variegated or hand-dyed scarlet (V028) [7] (carp heads)

7mm silk ribbon
- 5m (5½yd) natural white [8] (fish scales)

10mm (⅜in) silk ribbon
- 4m (4½yd) natural white [9] (fish scales)

13mm silk ribbon
- 4m (4½yd) natural white [10] (fish scales)

Order of work

Read the Getting started chapter on page 8 before beginning. Make a printed panel for this design (see the Designs to transfer section, page 196). My advice for working this design is to stitch one of the fish completely first so that you get the hang of it (the best choice is the solitary fish at the bottom). Then start working on the rest of the design, embroidering the same part for all of the fish before moving on to the next step. This will help speed up the job.

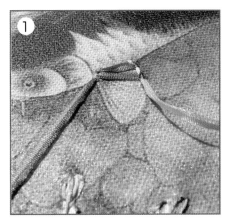 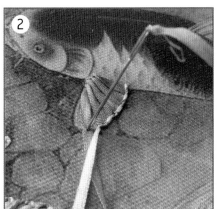 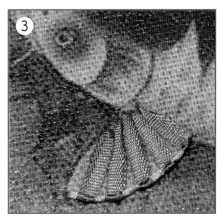

Carp fins

1 Step 1, pictures 1–3: 2mm taupe ribbon [5]. Victoria Amazonica technique worked with two no. 26 chenille needles (one for stitching ribbon, the other for supporting ribbon). Work stitches in taupe ribbon leaving some gaps in between them.

Step 2, picture 4: 2mm light yellow ribbon [4]. The same technique. Fill out the gaps left in the first step.

Photo 6 shows a part of the fin that is raised above the fish body. Work this part when you have finished embroidering the body. Raise the supporting ribbon to shape the fin (embroider that part of the fin with Raised ribbon stitches).

Step 3, pictures 7–9: 2mm variegated olive ribbon [6]. Twisted straight stitch. The aim of this step is to add texture. The stitches are spaced evenly along every fin.

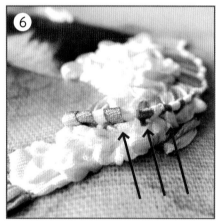

Fish scales

2 7mm, 10mm and 13mm natural white ribbon [8], [9], [10]. White stranded cotton thread. Zigzag gathering. Divide the length of a fish body into three equal parts. Use 7mm ribbon to stitch the tail part, then change to 10mm ribbon to work the middle part and finish with 13mm ribbon for the last part near the head. If you do this, Zigzag gathering by itself will shape the fish body, making the tail part the finest and the head part the most dimensional. The rows of the gathering should come across the fish body to imitate the body shape. Work each subsequent row to be half-overlapping the previous one.

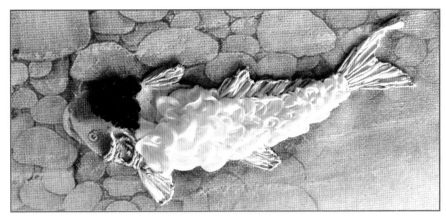

TIP

You will have to work the gathering along more than a dozen metres (yards) of silk ribbon, and it is important that the stitch line comes right up to the selvedge (diagram A). To speed up the job, go over the ribbon selvedge (diagram B).

A

B

Start from the tail of the third fish. First work Rudbeckia stitch along the tail fin. Go to the back of the fabric and come very close to the top side again. Now work the first row of Zigzag gathering with 7mm ribbon, stitching as many Zigzag scallops as are needed for each row. Do not come to the back of your embroidery at the end of each row: just fold the ribbon to start the next row (photo 1). Photo 2 and its inset picture show that each subsequent row goes in the opposite direction. To attach a stitched row to the fabric, work tiny Stab stitches with the same thread used for gathering.

Next stitch the middle third of the fish. Zigzag gathering with 10mm ribbon (photo 3).

Now stitch the head end of the fish. Zigzag gathering with 13mm ribbon (photo 4). Work a few rows of the gathering in the way described above. The last row is different. Having worked the usual gathering, fold the gathered ribbon in half lengthwise so that both rows of scallops overlap each other (you do not want any scallops covering the fish head).

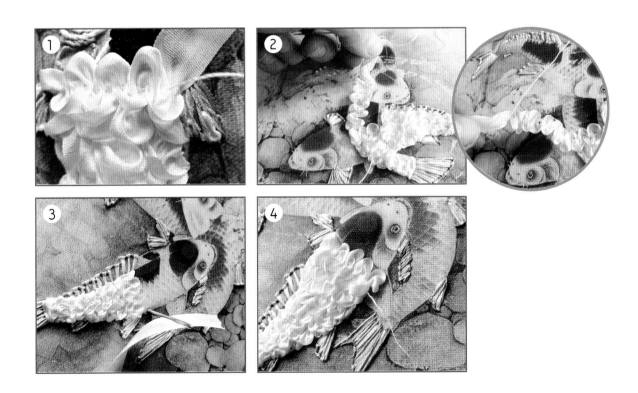

Carp heads

3 2mm black, crimson, variegated crimson and peach ribbon [1], [2], [3], [7], toning thread. Use Lazy ruche technique to speed up the embroidery of the carp heads. Use toning thread to fix the gathered ribbon on the fabric. Change the ribbon colour according to the colourful spots on the heads as shown in the printed panel.

 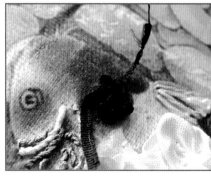 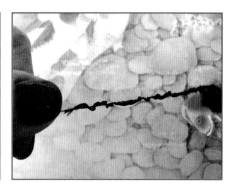

Fish gills

4 2mm crimson, peach and taupe ribbon [2], [1], [5] and grey DMC pearl cotton thread. Whipped backstitch, worked along the gill lines. Add some stripes of your own for decoration.

Trapunto for the carp heads

5 Grey stranded cotton thread or DMC pearl cotton thread size 8. Backstitch or Split stitch. See Trapunto embroidery on page 49. The only difference here is that the linen fabric is NOT attached to the fish body along the gills (the dotted green line in the photograph, left). Use this opening to fill in the 'pocket' between the two fabrics with felting wool, cotton wool or any other soft material.

Dyeing the fish

6 Dyeing the carp is really necessary as they seem to have turned into white sheep at this stage! Watercolour paints work fine. Apply some clean water to the area you are going to dye. Mix colours on the palette to get the right shade. Apply some paint to the fish and use a hairdryer to speed up the drying process.

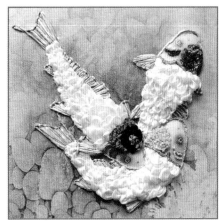 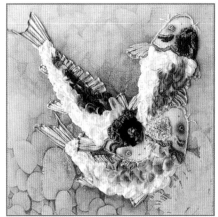

Thread embroidery details

Carp whiskers

7a White silk thread. Straight stitch, Lazy daisy stitch. Just mark the whiskers, work a few stitches and whip them to add texture.

Bubbles/ripples

7b White silk thread. Crochet chain. Use a 4mm crochet hook to create chain loops big enough to show the openwork of the water splashes. Work several chains 15cm (6in) long and attach them to the fabric with thread tails dangling from the two chain ends.

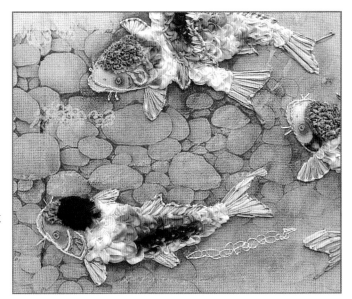

The fish can be worked as individual pieces and made into gifts.

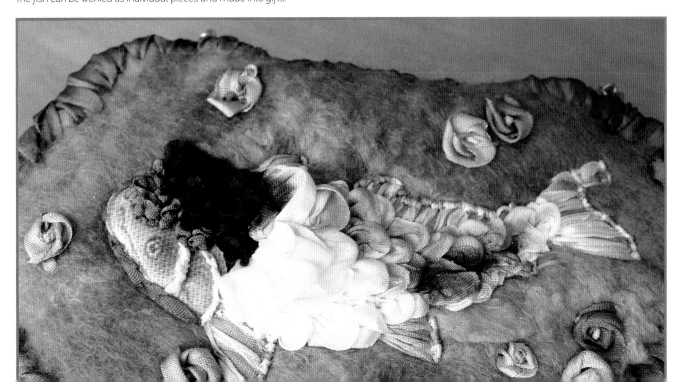

Christmas Star

The design is not an accurate portrait of the Star of Bethlehem, of course, just an artistic impression!

Finished size: 25 x 25cm (10 x 10in)

Skill level: Intermediate

Stitches used:

Twisted straight stitch
Rope technique
Ribbon stitch
Zigzag gathering
Cherry blossom gathering
Triangles in a square technique
Right angle technique
Goose foot technique
Pistil stitch

YOU WILL NEED

Stranded cotton thread in white

Beads, seed beads, pearls, findings, artificial flower stamens

Needles
- Chenille needles: no.16 for ropes worked in 2mm ribbon); no. 18 for 7mm ribbon; no. 26 for 2mm ribbon
- No. 10 straw needle for thread stitching

Bright white silk or atlas fabric with lustre (not matt) with trasferred template, see opposite, or find the kit for this design listed as K-060 'Christmas Star' on the author's website (see page 4)

2mm silk ribbon
- 2m (2¼yd) mustard (S660) [1] (leaves)

- 2m (2¼yd) taupe (S665) [2] (leaves)
- 2m (2¼yd) cornflower blue (S588) [3] (leaves)
- 7m (7¾yd) bright white [4] (twigs)

7mm silk ribbon
- 1.2m (47½in) mustard (S660) [5] (leaves)
- 1.2m (47½in) taupe (S665) [6] (leaves)
- 1.2m (47½in) cornflower blue (S588) [7] (leaves)

20mm silk ribbon
- 1m (39½in) hand-dyed bright blue [8] (buds)

25mm silk ribbon
- 2m (2¼yd) bright white [9] (big white flowers)
- 80cm (31½in) hand-dyed pale blue [10] (buds)

32mm silk ribbon
- 1.5m (59in) hand-dyed blue [11] (big blue flowers)

Order of work

Read the Getting started chapter on page 8 before beginning. Enlarge the template below to 200%, to give you the correct size, with a diameter of 25cm (10in). Transfer it onto your fabric. The work order for this design is not fixed, but it is recommended that you embroider the big blue flowers first.

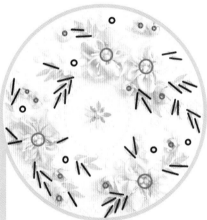

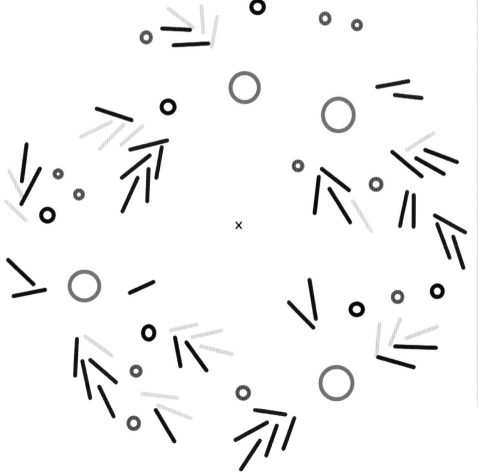

Key

The template is placed on top of the faded photograph for clarity.

- *Blue circles: the centres of the big blue flowers*
- *Dark grey circles: the centres of the big white flowers*
- *Orange circles: flower buds*
- *Yellow lines: leaves in mustard ribbon*
- *Brown lines: leaves in taupe ribbon*
- *Dark blue lines: leaves in cornflower blue ribbon*
- *X: the centre of the design*

The fine twigs are not marked. Do not mark them on the fabric as it will be difficult to hide the marks with embroidery.

Large blue flowers

1 32mm hand-dyed blue ribbon [11]. Cherry blossom gathering. Four flowers in a wreath. Work the gathering, leaving about 6cm (2¼in) space between the peaks. For a five-petal flower, cut a ribbon length according to the calculation:

(5 petals x 6cm/2¼in) + 2cm (¾in) ribbon tail allowance (to hide them under the petals) = about 32cm (12½in) ribbon per flower.

Stitch one flower first to see if you are happy with the result. If you want your flower petals to be puffier, increase the space between the peaks.

Flower centres are worked using beads, seed beeds and artificial stamens. String the beads onto the stamen thread. The rich colours of hand-dyed silk ribbon will inspire you to be creative!

Large white flowers

2 25mm white ribbon [9]. Zigzag gathering, Right angle technique. You will need about 30cm (12in) length of ribbon for one flower. There are six flowers of this kind in the original design. Working the Running stitch, do not forget to anchor the thread properly at the beginning of the stitch line (photo 1). Try to keep a 45 degree angle between the line of the running stitch and the ribbon selvage (the green dotted line in the diagram right). Widen the zigzags to get bigger petals (the yellow lines in photo 2).

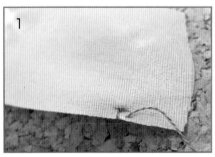
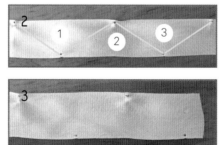

Work ten up-and-down paths of Zigzag gathering to get four triangles above the stitch line and five under it (the figures in orange and navy blue). The base of each triangle is about 5cm (2in) long. To make the triangles equal, mark the dots along both ribbon selvedges for the peaks, either using a water-soluble fabric marker or by piercing holes with your sewing needle (see photo 3). Pull on the thread to gather your ribbon and circle the gathered ribbon to make a flower with four petals on one side and five on the other. Attach it to the fabric using the Right angle technique.

Blue buds

3 20mm and 25mm hand-dyed ribbon of different shades of blue [8], [10]. Triangles in a square method. You will need about 13cm (5⅛in) ribbon for each flower. Follow the instructions for Triangles in a square. Attach it to the fabric, hiding the ribbon tails behind the petals. Change the placement of smaller and bigger buds, working them from different size ribbon: five bigger buds in 25mm ribbon and six smaller ones in 20mm ribbon.

Leaves

4 2mm and 7mm cornflower blue, mustard and taupe ribbon [1], [2], [3], [5], [6], [7]. Ribbon stitch, Goose foot technique. For each leaf, work a Centre ribbon stitch using 7mm ribbon. Now change to a toning 2mm ribbon and make the three shorter Ribbon stitches fanning out at the base of the 7mm Ribbon stitch. In this way, you Stab stitch the base of the 7mm Ribbon stitch and both ribbon selvedges.

Fine white twigs

5 2mm bright white ribbon [4]. Twisted straight stitch and Rope method. Cut a 50cm (20in) length of ribbon and attach one end to something such as your pincushion using a sewing pin. Twist the other ribbon end tightly (as for Twisted straight stitch). Make sure your ribbon remains stretched while you are twisting it. Fold the ribbon in half and let its parts twirl around each other to produce a fine rope that is twisted evenly and smoothly. Remove the pin and knot both ribbon tails together to prevent the rope from untwisting.

Thread the rope into a no. 16 or 18 chenille needle and bring it to the right side of your embroidery at the base of a twig. Unthread the needle. Work out any intricate pattern with your rope, Stab stitching it now and then using one strand of white stranded cotton thread. Try to hide the thread stitches inside the rope twists. To do this, come to the right side of the fabric close to the rope and then go down through the rope. Go on working until you reach the rope tip. Attach the tip in a similar way. Scatter these fine twisted twigs evenly around the design but be sure to leave some free space in between them to add some 'air'. As they say, there is beauty in empty space!

Decorative beads

6 Having finished the work, take out your bead treasures to see what fits your design. Scatter them around the design until you are happy with the result and then attach them using a toning thread or a special thread for beading.

Create your own decorations to add texture. The rays around the Star in the centre are Pistil stitches worked in 2mm white ribbon.

January Cup

This is part of the 12 Cups series (see page 139). A large part of the Eastern Orthodox Church observes Christmas Day according to the Julian rather than the Gregorian calendar. This means celebrating Christmas on January 7th, so New Year's Day comes before Christmas. A fir tree is decorated on New Year's Eve and kept until Christmas. This is celebrated in this design.

Skill level: Beginner

Finished size: 19 x 22.5cm (7½ x 8¾in)

YOU WILL NEED

Stranded cotton thread
- Dark green (holly leaves)

Needles
- Chenille needles: no. 20 for 4mm and 7mm ribbon and no. 26 for 2mm ribbon and thread

Piece of fabric with printed panel for embroidery, see page 206, or find the kit for this design listed as K-065 '12 Cups, January' on the author's website (see page 4)

Beads and sequins

2mm silk ribbon
- 30cm (12in) saffron yellow (J054) [1] (bows)
- 3m (3½yd) moss green (S658) [2] (New Year tree)
- 4m (4½yd) dark green (J021) [3] (New Year tree)

4mm silk ribbon
- 40cm (15¾in) saffron yellow (J054) [4] (bows)
- 2m (79in) scarlet (S539) [5] (holly berries)

7mm silk ribbon
- 60cm (23½in) saffron yellow (J054) [6] (bows)
- 2m (79in) dark green (J021) [7] (holly leaves)

Stitches used:

Straight stitch
Arched straight stitch
Couched straight stitch
Twisted straight stitch
Arched ribbon stitch
Lazy daisy stitch
French knots
Small bow stitch

Order of work

Read the Getting started chapter on page 8 before beginning. Make a printed panel for this design (see the Designs to transfer section, page 196).

New Year tree

1 2mm moss green and dark green. Twisted straight stitch. Use dark green ribbon first to stitch the needles of all the branches of this conifer. Now change to moss green to fill in the spaces between the previous stitches. Move from the top to the bottom of the tree while stitching.

Holly leaves

2 7mm dark green ribbon. Dark green stranded cotton thread. Arched straight stitch, Arched ribbon stitch, Lazy daisy stitch, Couched straight stitch. Work an arched stitch of either kind and press it flat onto the fabric, pulling on its selvedges to the right and then left. Stab stitch the scallops to create a natural holly leaf shape.

TIP

Work the fixing of the scallops in two steps: first Stab stitch them and work the central leaf veins in Couched straight stitches. Then work a Lazy daisy stitch for each scallop tip using one strand of stranded cotton thread.

Holly berries

3 4mm scarlet ribbon. One-wrap French knots. Note that the printed panel shows fewer berries than the finished design. This is because you can add as many as you want!

Bows

4 2mm, 4mm and 7mm saffron yellow ribbon. Small bow stitch, Straight stitch. Work bows in 7mm ribbon and Stab stitch their loops using 2mm ribbon. Slide a piece of 4mm ribbon inside the 7mm Straight stitch of a bow, so that the ribbon tails appear on both sides of it. To prevent fraying, make V-shaped cuts in the ribbon: fold the ribbon in half lengthwise and start your cut where the ribbon ends come together. Cut slanting up and away from the end. Now you should have a V or inverted V shape in your ribbon ends.

TIP

You will be more comfortable with these tiny bows and small ribbon tails if you work as follows:
1) Work the first V-cut.
2) Insert the ribbon inside the 7mm Straight stitch of the bow.
At this point you can also work an additional Stab stitch with 4mm ribbon around the bow's knot.
3) Finish the job, making another V-cut in the second ribbon end.

Decorating the New Year tree

5 Select beads and sequins to decorate the New Year tree and make garlands.
Sparkling Swarovski crystals will also work wonderfully. Just make sure the decorations
are not too big for the tree. For the garlands, use beads of at least two colours.

What to make with the embroidery

This is for you to decide. You could make it into a wall-hanging, a pillow case or
anything else you can think of. It would make a lovely gift for New Year, or could
decorate your house at this time of year.

Designs to transfer

Use the iron transfer method to transfer pictures onto fabric, creating printed panels ready for embroidery. You will need light cotton fabric, iron transfer paper (also called heat transfer paper) for light cotton fabric, an image to transfer, an iron and ironing board.

There are many types of iron transfer paper: for inkjet or laser printers, for light or dark fabric, and for use with an iron or a heat press (available at some print/copy centres).

First, choose which type of printer you will use. Laser transfers are usually considered to be of higher quality than inkjet transfers, especially for use on T-shirts etc. However, inkjet printers have a definite advantage when creating printed panels for embroidery: the transfer paper for these printers is finer and easier to stitch over. On the other hand, iron transfers made with laser printers are more durable and that is important if you are creating an item such as a bag or pillow case.

You definitely need the transfer paper for light fabric. The dark option is for T-shirts and other kinds of clothes. If you are going to make a transfer at home, choose the one for ironing. If you would like to go to a print/copy centre, buy paper for heat press.

You will find pictures to create the printed panels for the designs in this book on the following pages. Scan or photograph the image. Scanning is preferable as you will not get any distortions of shape or colour. Most of the images from the book are full size, but check the original size in the project instructions. Of course you can reduce or enlarge the images if you prefer.

You can also use the designs in the book for inspiration only and use the embroidery techniques on a design of your own choice. Choose an image of the highest resolution possible, although lower resolution will not spoil the quality of a printed panel as much as it might for a T-shirt, as you will cover the whole image with stitching and thus add the absent details and clarity.

The pictures on the following pages are already mirror images ready for transfer. If you are using your own pictures, you need to make mirror images of them before transferring. Use any program which works with jpg images and choose the option 'make a mirror image'.

Print the image, making sure you print it on the blank, sticky side of iron transfer paper, not on the checked/marked side!

Cut a piece of fabric at least 10cm (4in) wider and longer than your image. It should fit your embroidery hoop or frame. Iron the fabric: rinse it with water first or just steam iron it.

Make sure the fabric is well ironed and completely dry. Any damp spots may totally spoil the transfer. Place your image onto the fabric with the photograph facing the fabric, ready to iron the side which is checked or otherwise marked. Heat your iron to the maximum temperature (or follow the instructions that come with your iron transfer paper). Remember you want no steam for this! Start ironing, working with your iron on top of the paper-and-fabric sandwich, making circular movements. You would normally iron an A4 size sheet of paper for about two minutes. Pay special attention to the border and the corners of the paper: slow down your ironing movements at those spots and work over them repeatedly, or let the iron sit there without moving for a couple of seconds.

Iron transfer paper consists of the two layers: fine film at the blank side and the protective layer, usually marked or checked. Most manufacturers produce iron-on paper with a protective layer that is supposed to be removed when your fabric has cooled down after ironing. In that case it will come off easily. However, some types have a protective layer to be removed while the transfer is still hot/warm. Check your transfer paper's instructions.

Your printed panel is now complete! Just fix it in your embroidery hoop or frame and start stitching. Make sure your frame is bigger than the size of the printed panel, otherwise you may damage the panel.

TIP

Sometimes it is recommended to use a hard board rather than a soft-padded ironing board for making iron-on transfers. Have a try to see if you are happy with the results. Also they say the heavier your iron, the easier it will be to transfer the image.

Your Day project, page 94

Opposite: *From Olga's Garden project, page 102*   **Above:** *Meadow Posy project, page 114*   **Below:** *Christmas Rose project, page 134*

Above:

Sunny Road project, page 130

Opposite:

Autumn Biasket project, page 120

Above:

Mother's Day project, page 158

Opposite:

February Cup project, page 138

August Cup
project, page 164

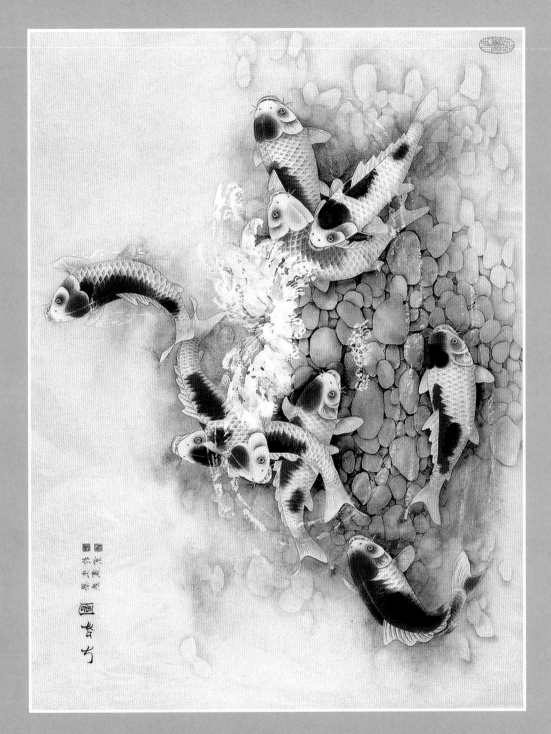

House-warming Carp project, page 182.

Please note, this image is shown half size. Enlarge it
to 200% before trasferring it to your fabric.

Stitch index

Arched ribbon stitch 25
Arched straight stitch 21

Backstitch 45
Belt technique 38
Big bow stitch 24
Braid technique 57
Bow on a fork technique 37
Buttonhole stitch 47
Button rose technique (or Flat
  rose) 43

Cabbage leaf technique 38
Centre ribbon stitch 25
Chain stitch 46
Cherry blossom (or Sakura)
  gathering 35
Classical twisted rose 37
Colonial knot 32
Couched straight stitch 23
Crescent rose 23
Crochet chain 48

Double ribbon stitch 27
Double tent technique 39

Eyelash technique 52
Eye-looped stitch 21

False bullion knot technique 60
Feather stitch 31
Flood filling technique 57
Fly stitch 29
Folded ribbon stitch 28
Folded straight stitch 23
French knot 31

Goose foot technique 61
Grab stitch 29
Great Wall of China technique 56

Half-bow stitch 27
Half-cabbage leaf technique 39
Hemisphere technique 59
Hood technique 61

Jabot gathering 34

Knotted daisy stitch 30
Knotted flowers 42
Kokeshi doll technique 53

Lazy daisy stitch (classical) 29
Lazy double ruche technique 55
Lazy ruche technique 54
Lazy tuning fork technique 60
Long and short stitch 46
Loop (or looped straight stitch) 21
Looped ribbon stitch 25
Looped straight stitch (or a loop) 21
Low hill sakura 36

One slope sakura 36
Open chain stitch 46
Open fishbone stitch 47

Padded straight stitch 23
Pistil stitch 31
Plume stitch 24
Plumeria technique 56
Puffy petals 44

Raised ribbon stitch (or ribbon
  stitch on a stem) 28
Raised stem stitch 46
Reverse ribbon stitch 26
Ribbon plus technique 50
Ribbon stitch (centre ribbon
  stitch) 25
Ribbon stitch on a stem (or raised
  ribbon stitch) 28
Right angle technique 62
Rope rose (or twirled ribbon
  rose) 22
Rope technique 22
Rounded slope sakura 36
Ruche gathering 34
Rudbeckia ribbon stitch 28
Running stitch 45

Side (right or left) ribbon stitch 27
Small bow stitch 24
Spider web rose 30
Split stitch 46
Star rose 32
Stem stitch 45
Straight stitch 21

Tassel stitch 47
Tent technique 38
There-and-back technique 55
Trapunto embroidery 49
Triangles in a square technique 40
Tuning fork stitch 49
Twirled ribbon rose 22
Twisted daisy stitch 29
Twisted ribbon stitch 26
Twisted straight stitch 22
Two-sided Janus technique 41

Vertical line technique 61
Victoria Amazonica technique 51

Wasp waist technique 56
Weaving stitch 47
Whipped backstitch 45
Whipped chain stitch 46
Whipped running stitch 45
Whipped straight stitch 23
Whipped stem stitch 45
Whipstitch finishing 58
Wide ribbon rosebud 39
Woven circle filling needlelace 48

Zigzag gathering 35

Flower index

Cherry blossom 35
Chrysanthemum 130, *201*

Daffodil 34, 138–141, *202*
Dahlia 153
Daisy 77, 114–119, *199*
Delphinium 165, 167

Helebore 134, 136, 137, *199*

Lily of the valley 59, 90–93

Nasturtium 25, 129

Pansy 60, 95–97, 99–101, *197*
Peony 176, 178, 179
Primrose 138, 139, 141, 142, 176, 179, *202*

Rose 17, 22, 23, 29, 30, 32, 37, 39, 43, 77, 102, 104–113, 158, 160, 161, 172–175, *198, 203*

Sunflower 120, 121, 123–125, 127, 165, 166, *200, 204*

Numbers in italic refer to pictures for transferring to fabric.